LESSONS IN **LOVE, LOSS,** AND **RECOVERY**

LEGACY

L*of*OVE

"because of him I know love"

DEBBIE GORDON

Publishing Services provided by Paper Raven Books

Printed in the United States of America

First Printing, 2021

Paperback ISBN= 978-1-7360103-0-3
Hardback ISBN= 978-1-7360103-1-0

DEDICATION

**To the friends and
family of Larry James Borg**

SERENITY PRAYER

God grant me the serenity
To accept the things I cannot change,
Courage to change the things I can
And the wisdom to know the difference.
Living one day at a time,
Enjoying one moment at a time;
Accepting hardship as a pathway to peace;
Taking, as Jesus did,
This sinful world as it is,
Not as I would have it:
Trusting that You will make all things right
If I surrender to Your will;
So that I may be reasonably happy in this life
And supremely happy with You forever in the next.
Amen

Reinhold Niebuhr[1]

ACKNOWLEDGMENT

I would like to thank my friends for their encouragement and support as I began writing this book. Thank you for listening and for encouraging me to continue writing. I know that it was God who inspired my hands as I wrote. Blue Mountain Academy will remain special to me, as it's the place where I wrote this book. To all the individuals who lived there during the short period I was there, I extend my deepest thanks. Your support and strength provided me with courage to live again. I would also like to extend my deepest gratitude to my friend Cathy, who took my broken, incoherent thoughts and made them sparkle and become the story that I have today. Thank you also to Dinah, Rachel, and my writing group, who provided feedback and encouragement. And thank you to my amazing team at Paper Raven Books, who made this twenty-eight-year dream finally become a reality. To all of you who helped make this book possible by reading it, editing it, or just listening to it, I thank you. I found incredible healing writing this book. It is my hope that all who read it may discover inspiration, encouragement, and healing, and it is my prayer that God will utilize this book to touch everyone's life in a very special way.

CONTENTS

Preface   1

Fall Quarter I

1. A Special Place   3
2. Introductions   9
3. Winter Quarter Loneliness   13
4. Emilia   19
5. Larry   21

Winter Quarter I

6. Sledding Escapades   25
7. Burman Hall   33
8. A Spring Walk   37

Spring Quarter I

9. A Dinner Invitation   45
10. Spring Fever   51
11. Larry's Offer   59
12. The 5k Race   65
13. English Competition   71
14. Pictionary   77
15. A Willing Subject   81

16. Roommate Problems   87
17. A Failed Exam   91
18. A Simple Prayer   95

Fall Quarter II

19. A New School Year   105
20. The Dunes   113
21. Philosophical Thoughts   117
22. Class Assignments   121
23. Extreme Exhaustion   127
24. Mono   133
25. A Compliment   139
26. Lauren   143
27. Microbiology Cultures   147
28. A Special Birthday   149
29. Goodbyes   159

Winter Quarter II

30. Home Again   167

Spring Quarter II

31. Beauty and the Beast   173
32. An Answered Prayer   181
33. The Mystery Bird   185
34. Grape Juice   187
35. A Tennis Date   191

36.	Telephone Operator	197
37.	Gifts	201
38.	A Surprise Birthday Party	209
39.	Surprises	215

Summer Quarter II

40.	Camille	219
41.	A Special Family	227
42.	Letters	229

Fall Quarter III

43.	Friendship Blossoms	233
44.	Larry's Gifts	241
45.	Floral Surprise	249
46.	Racquetball and a Photograph	253
47.	Thomas	257
48.	Dreams	261
49.	The St. Joseph Pier	267

Conclusion	273
Epilogue	289
Eulogy	295
Letter to Larry	305
Soulmates	311
Afterword	313
References	315

PREFACE

Memories.

The mere mention of this word evokes many feelings. Memories may lead to happy, blissful thoughts and yet, in the same moment, may also arouse feelings of sadness and grief. How can it be possible to feel happiness and sorrow simultaneously? The unique way in which emotions are intertwined in our memories, in our entire being, is uncanny. They mold each of us into unique individuals. Each person has their own memories, specific to that person. Even individuals experiencing a similar situation recall and express it in different ways. One moment or event may be equated with joyful, pleasant memories for some and painful, aching memories for others. The way we store our recollections displays the incredible creativity that God had in His mind when He designed us. This specialness makes life rich and wonderful. The individual way everyone perceives and evaluates experiences adds the spark of difference to our world, imbuing variety to the flavor of the friendships that we form.

My friends are extremely special to me. Their uniqueness, their support, their laughter, and all else that encompass friendship—phrases, idiosyncrasies, facial expressions, quirks, beliefs, values, songs—are treasures that I cherish in each person I meet. All my friends are dear to me, because each of them, in their own way, teaches me things that I would otherwise never come to know. Even people that I've only been acquainted with for a few months will enter my mind occasionally, and I can't help wondering how they're doing. At these times, a prayer escapes and I ask God to protect and lead them.

This uniqueness, this individuality, is what I wish to portray as I describe my friend Larry Borg, for it was his personality and his uniqueness that I admired. After I became acquainted with him, part of me changed as he shared his individuality with me. How could I ever forget his specialness, his friendship? This is a story about my friend as I will always remember him. His life held an example that all of us may learn from. As I remember Larry, memories lead me through the experiences we shared. How could I ever forget the enthusiasm and cheer that he added to my life and others that he touched? This is his story, his legacy of love.

A SPECIAL PLACE

I t was my junior year of college at Andrews University, a Seventh-day Adventist college in Berrien Springs, Michigan. Returning to the school was exciting, but I was also apprehensive. Resuming my studies at Andrews was difficult. As a sophomore, I had studied Spanish at a gorgeous school in Sagunto, Spain, where the climate was hot and sunny the majority of the year. Michigan was quite different, as the temperatures started to drop in early fall and winters were snowy and cold. Additionally, all the friends with whom I regularly associated during my freshman year lived off campus, and being shy, I was worried about making new friends. As an introvert, I was terrified to enter the cafeteria alone. Whenever I entered the cafeteria by myself, a knot formed in my stomach, almost making me nauseous. At my age, I knew I should be past these feelings, but somehow, I never seemed to outgrow the anxiety that I always felt going into a crowded place with unfamiliar faces. This lack of courage bothered me.

Being away the year before made me nervous and my anxiety caused me to momentarily consider not returning to Andrews my junior year, especially as I'd have to make new friends. However, my fears dissipated when I learned about a new speech and hearing clinic that was opening at the university. I had taken classes in speech pathology during my freshman year and had talked about my interest in this field with my aunt and uncle. My uncle was the administrator of a hospital that owned the university's speech and hearing clinic, and he knew the professors. It was my aunt's gentle yet earnest prodding that convinced me to consider returning to Andrews that autumn so I could tour the clinic and pursue the new and exciting opportunity.

So, there I was again in the petite town of Berrien Springs, driving up to Andrews University, fighting the apprehension of facing new people and new situations. Fortunately, that year I was blessed with having a car of my own, and as I drove up to the campus again, I realized that I had honestly missed the area. In my year away, I'd forgotten about how charming a town Berrien Springs actually was and how beautiful the campus and its surroundings were. The school was located in a very small town situated about three miles away from the main street, where a small chain of stores sat, including a grocery store, post office, florist, pharmacy, and Chinese restaurant. Berrien was a town of orchards and farms interspersed with a few stores, homes, and enormous farmsteads with fields of thriving produce and orchards filled with mouth-watering peaches and apples. The site was breathtaking, especially in the autumn and spring. Bright, fiery leaves interspersed with splotches of gold and green in the autumn filled the air with splendor. Spring was also beautiful and richly abundant with hues of lavender and mauve from the newly forming blossoms. I can still smell the wonderful fragrances they brought.

As a nature-loving person, I thought the setting of the university was perfect for my taste. I loved the peace and quiet that could easily be discovered in the woods and fields beyond the university. It was so peaceful. It would be a heavenly refuge from the stresses of studying. I was glad to be back, and as I drove up, I felt fortunate to be attending that fall in spite of my concerns and fears. Andrews University was very different from public universities. At many colleges, stores are easily accessible from campus either by walking or by some convenient form of public transportation. At Andrews, the traveling distance was not always convenient, especially given the busy, hectic schedules of college students. Berrien was a rural area and malls and other stores were not close by, so my car would be a blessing and make it more convenient to travel to stores and to work.

The university had separate dorms for men and women. In my junior year, I was residing in the women's dormitory, Lamson Hall. The men's dorms, Meier Hall and Burman Hall, were visible just across the football field. As a private university, Andrews had some regulations not found at public colleges. All of the dorm residents were required to attend between five and eight worship services per week in their dorm. The number of worships depended on the class standing of the student, with freshman students required to attend the most worships and graduate students the fewest. On top of this, all of the students were obligated to attend chapel on Tuesdays and assembly on Fridays. If there was a conflict with work, the student had to petition for approval by the university staff. Faith and worship were one of the cornerstones of our education.

The consumption of alcohol, a problem at most universities, was not permitted on our campus. If an individual was caught with an alcoholic beverage, they would be suspended from the school. The strict penalties meant that there were not the abuses that are so often prevalent on campuses where alcohol is allowed. Smoking was also prohibited, and I was thankful for that rule because I suffered from asthma.

The school was founded on Biblical beliefs. One belief was that the seventh day, Saturday, was God's special day of worship. Like that of the Jewish faith, the Sabbath began when the sun set on Friday night and ended when the sun set on Saturday night. Sabbath was always my favorite day of the week, a day to relax from the frenzied pace of life. It was a day to recover from the tremendous pressures of the week, leave all of the worries and cares of life behind, and rest and worship the Lord.

The tiny size of the campus led to the forming of many friendships. Little did I know then just how important this university and the people I met would be to me in the years to come.

2

INTRODUCTIONS

The petite size of the campus was perfect for me, especially after attending small private schools all my life. I would have been overwhelmed by the size of a public university! Because the school was so small, it was easy to become familiarized with many names and faces. Gradually, my horizon of friendships grew as I was introduced to many women living in my dorm and to people in the cafeteria. One individual I became acquainted with that fall was Larry Borg. He was one of my classmates in an introductory course to psychology, but we weren't formally introduced until several weeks into the quarter. My roommate, Maria, and I meandered over to the action-packed student center for a break. Bubbly and outgoing, Maria initiated a conversation with a student she knew. They were deeply engrossed in conversation, and it took me some time to realize that it was the same student I'd been admiring in class for weeks. Maria formally introduced us.

"Are you taking Psychology 101?" Larry asked, looking intently at me.

Evidently, Larry had noticed me in psychology class as well. For a few brief moments, my mind digressed to images and thoughts about Larry. Something drew me to him. I couldn't help watching him in class. He typically sat in the very front aisle seat on the left side of the room. He possessed a cheery smile, and there was a radiant sparkle in his blue eyes. Larry stood over six feet tall and towered over my short stature, which measured just barely over five feet tall. He had curly, reddish-brown hair, and a ruddy complexion on his cheeks imparted a healthy glow. His round, wire-rimmed glasses bestowed an intelligent appearance, which he confirmed daily when he asked questions or expanded on statements that our professor made in class. Larry struck me as the type of person who earned good grades without tremendous effort. I always envied those people!

Hastily, I pulled my mind back to Larry's question. "Yes, I am," I said, smiling.

Larry and I discussed a reading assignment that was due that week in our class. Somehow my shyness melted away when I was talking to him. He was so easy to talk to, and time slipped away quickly. Maria and

I didn't stay long though. After a few more minutes passed, Maria and I walked back to our dorm to resume our studies. I didn't talk to Larry much more until one day when our professor requested that we form groups to discuss a reading assignment in class. Larry lingered, observing which group I joined before approaching. I talked briefly to him after we completed our assignment.

"What are you majoring in?" I asked him.

"I'm pre-physical therapy," he said. "I'm a freshman this year, and I have to complete the course requirements before I'm accepted into the program."

It seemed like a good major for the studious person I envisioned him being.

"What are you studying?" Larry asked me.

"Speech pathology," I replied not realizing at the time how our career choices were so interconnected. We were both majoring in the rehabilitation field.

Talking to him was easy and natural, even for the shy, timid person I was. Somehow his sanguine, phlegmatic spirit caused me to relax. I was never nervous around Larry. It felt like we'd known each other forever. In the brief times I'd spoken with him, I knew I could talk to him about anything and he'd listen. His personality caused my shyness and insecurities to evaporate. It felt so natural talking to him!

After that, the quarter was busy and our interactions were sparse, but one warm sunny Sabbath afternoon that fall, I traveled to the beach with friends and Larry joined me. That beautiful day blue skies filled the horizon as we enjoyed playing frisbee, walking along the beach, and splashing in the waves. We had an enjoyable time hanging out with our friends, but the memory that I will always cherish is when Larry and another man named Kevin decided to make a chair with their arms. My friends placed me on the top and somebody snapped a picture. I treasure this photograph of that special time to this very day.

After that, the quarter passed by rapidly and I was swamped in mounds of schoolwork. The pressure of projects needing to be completed that fall kept me occupied for the remainder of that quarter. My interactions with Larry were brief, even in our psychology class. He must have been just as busy that quarter as I was.

3

WINTER QUARTER LONELINESS

A s I entered the sanctuary and walked down the red carpeted aisles of the large stone campus church, Pioneer Memorial Church on that first Sabbath of winter quarter, sun streamed through the stained-glass windows. The long oval lights hanging from the ceiling added a warm glow to the wooden architecture of the gabled, triangular, sloped ceiling and wooden beams on the church walls. The wooden pews were filled with people, but the crowd was sparser than normal as it was the beginning of the quarter. Organ music reverberated from the walls of the church as I sat down. I still remember the sermon the pastor preached that day. The sermon was about ministering to those who surround us by reaching out to offer cheer to each person we pass, by offering a friendly smile or hello, or just by taking time to talk to them.

Normally, Maria would have been sitting next to me, but she was returning late that semester as she was applying for her U.S. citizenship. Maria had finally received a court hearing, and she had to pass a test before she could proceed with the court date and be sworn in as an official American citizen. I was pleased for her, but it was a difficult time for me. I felt lost without my roommate, and I missed chatting with her. The room was so silent without her voice. It drove me crazy. I must have phoned home ten times while she was gone. I ached for someone to talk to, because although I had met people the previous quarter, I hadn't branched out and was still not well acquainted with very many people. My shyness impacted my ability to make friends, and I was so lonesome. The sermon was exactly what I needed to hear during this lonely time.

Listening to the pastor's sermon, my mind turned to a paper I'd written the previous quarter for religion class in which I had confronted the same issue. I described how Jesus ministered to everyone He encountered, and I discussed the importance of following Christ's example by reaching out just as the Good Samaritan did. Sitting on the wooden pews in church that day, I asked myself whether I was positively impacting others or whether I was too preoccupied with my own worries, loneliness, and shyness to minister to them. The pastor challenged us to pray that God would send someone to us that we could help. So, I prayed. I always ached to help others, but listening to the sermon provided me with an even stronger desire to reach out. As I prayed, I remembered a poem I'd read during my freshman year:

As I Go on My Way

My life will touch a dozen lives before
this day is done,
Leave countless marks for good or ill ere
sets the evening sun;
So, this the wish I always wish, the prayer
I ever pray,
Let my life help other lives it touches
by the way.

Strickland Gillilan[2]

With this poem in mind, I prayed that the Lord would use me to minister to others and that He would help me befriend someone. When we minister to others, God often blesses us as well. God used this sermon to teach me how to better minister to people, and in the process, He blessed me with an incredible friend. In time, my loneliness and shyness were removed through this amazing friendship. Maybe I didn't bless him as much as he blessed me, but ministry often serves as a twofold blessing.

Although winter quarter began with this amazing sermon and these prayers in the back of my mind, as so often happens, they were forgotten, as the busyness and stress of life took hold. My prayers shaped into asking God for strength to handle the pressures of that quarter, and the sermon and prayers were lost in the craziness of college life. Other concerns and issues took precedence in my daily prayers with God.

As a junior in college, I was discovering the profession that would allow me to work with children and more specifically children with hearing loss. It fulfilled a dream that developed from childhood and my great-grandmother's influence in my life. Despite her profound hearing loss and blindness, she had a positive outlook on life that inspired me and drew me to the field of speech-language pathology. The Lord knew exactly what I'd be most satisfied doing when He guided me to Andrews University that fall. I was honestly enjoying what I was learning as I was exposed to the field that had first captured my interest during sign language classes my freshman year. My interest and enthusiasm increased my motivation to succeed academically. I focused on studying for classes, writing papers, preparing for exams, and surviving another quarter.

~4~

EMILIA

One evening shortly after Maria returned, we were both studying in our dorm room when we heard someone nearby speaking in Spanish.

Suddenly, Maria turned to me and asked, "Did someone new move in next door?"

"I don't know," I said.

Maria listened for a few minutes, then she jumped up out of her chair with excitement. "Hey, she speaks like I do! I wonder where she's from. Let's go and meet her."

Our friend Anne joined us in the hall as we stood around, wondering if we should knock on the door or not. It sounded like the new student was talking on the phone. Finally, one of us worked up enough courage to knock. A short Hispanic woman with a friendly face and jet-black hair greeted us at the door. A phone receiver was on her ear when she opened the door.

"Just a minute," she said to the person on the phone, still holding the receiver as we introduced ourselves.

We learned that her name was Emilia and that her family was from El Salvador. She told us that she had spent the past few months in boot camp training as a medical assistant. Emilia continued to talk at length, barely taking a breath between sentences. Whomever Emilia was speaking with on the phone finally hung up, probably after realizing that Emilia was focused on talking to someone else. Finally, we, too, somehow managed to bring her narrative to a close.

When Maria and I returned to our dorm room, she told me that she was pleased to meet someone else from El Salvador. Being our next-door neighbor, Emilia was a frequent visitor. As the quarter progressed, we were often graced by Emilia's presence and we would frequently hear her rhythmic knocking on our door. It was a blessing, but at times it made it difficult for us to have the solitude we needed to study. Interruptions and all, she added variety to our lives, and humor and enthusiasm to our days. Life was never dull with Emilia's spunky, vibrant personality.

Part of the fun I had with Emilia stemmed from the fact that we were total opposites. I tended to be quiet around people I didn't know. Emilia, on the other hand, enjoyed talking and would talk to anyone, even if she didn't know the person. Extremely outgoing, Emilia loved being around people. She did not like silence and usually had music playing continually, which wore on my nerves. Reflecting on our differences, I wonder how we ever managed to get along. However, her outgoing side balanced out my introverted personality and helped improve my ability to talk to people and conquer some of my shyness.

Emilia also spoke in Spanish quite often, and I appreciated having an informal tutor. With her as my teacher, my Spanish improved. Often, we would tease each other about one another's accents. I was taking a class in phonetics, the study and classification of speech sounds, and so I began to listen more carefully to the way people spoke. When I pointed out the imperfections in Emilia's English, she would tease me about my "poor Spanish." I didn't mind. In fact, I was thankful, because she was helping me improve my Spanish. This would be an important skill in the years to come.

5

LARRY

One January evening, the phone rang unexpectedly in our dorm room and interrupted our studying.

"Hi, this is Larry. Am I bothering you?"

I was surprised to hear from Larry. We hadn't talked in weeks, and he had never called me before. I was flattered that he was thinking of me.

"No," I said, with a hint of curiosity.

"Are you busy?" Larry asked, clearly not wanting to disturb me if I was.

"I was just studying, but I could use a break."

"What are you studying?" he asked.

"Phonetics. I'm learning how to transcribe what people say. So far, I really like the class. What are you doing?"

"That sounds interesting," he said. "I'm just taking a break right now."

"What classes are you taking this quarter?" I asked him.

"My early class is Christ in Music and Art. That one is at seven in the morning, and I'm struggling to wake up early enough to make it to that class. My other classes are communications and the other general electives I need for my physical therapy major."

"Early morning classes definitely are hard," I said. "I'm glad I don't have many early morning classes. My classes are mostly in the morning but not typically that early. That would be difficult to stay awake in!"

"The biggest problem with the class is that the professor turns the lights out and shows slides," he replied. "I'm already tired, and with the lights out it's hard to stay awake."

"That would be tough. I'd fall asleep, too," I said. "That happens to me in my morning Bible class, because the teacher's voice almost puts me to sleep. Those are definitely tough classes."

There was a brief silence. Then I heard, "I sure wish it would snow so I could go sledding. I love sledding."

"That sounds like fun."

"It is! You'll have to go some time," he said.

"I'd like that."

We sat in silence for a moment as he seemed to be pondering a thought. Then he said, "It sure was nice to go home during Christmas vacation, because I got to see my horse. I miss my horse."

"Horses are nice," I said. "I loved the horses we rode when I was a kid. It was fun riding them with my cousins. They are a lot of fun."

The conversation continued as if we'd known each other forever. Larry's outgoing personality diminished my shyness. It was extremely easy to talk to him. We quickly became engrossed in conversation. He wasn't critical and didn't analyze everything I said, so I wasn't timid talking to him. His temperament put me at ease immediately, and the phone provided the one-on-one setting that alleviated my shyness.

"Do you mind if I call you again?" Larry asked at the end of our conversation.

"No, of course not," I said.

I was thankful Larry had called and pleased he had the courage to talk to somebody he hardly knew. I admired Larry for having the boldness to make that first phone call.

We were still talking when Maria returned a half hour later.

"Who was that?" Maria asked after we hung up.

"Larry," I said. "That was the first time he called me."

"What did he want?" Maria asked.

"Just to talk, I guess. He sounded lonesome. Maybe he just needs friends. Larry asked if he could call again, and of course I said yes. He was thoughtful and even asked if he was bothering me. People don't do that very often."

"That's great. He seems like a nice person," Maria said.

6

SLEDDING ESCAPADES

A few weeks after my first phone conversation with Larry, Maria and I were at our desks studying when the telephone rang. The one phone in our room was next to Maria's side of the desk, so she answered the call. I could hear Larry's voice from where I sat.

"This is Larry. Are you guys busy?"

"We were just studying," Maria said. "Why?"

"Well," he said, "it's a great evening to go sledding. I'm planning on going with a friend of mine. Would you and Debbie like to come along?"

"Where do you go sledding?" she asked.

"We usually go down Pathfinder Hill," Larry said enthusiastically. "It's a spectacular evening to go. The weather is perfect!"

Turning to me, Maria said, "Did you hear that? Larry wants to know if we'd like to go sledding down Pathfinder Hill. What do you think? It sounds kind of scary, huh?"

Larry assured us it was safe. He'd gone before and was anxious to go again. The thought of something different sounded exciting and there weren't any pressing assignments to be completed. After a brief conference, Maria told him we'd go.

"Meet me in the lobby of the student center in fifteen minutes," Larry said. "We'll sneak a couple extra trays out of the cafeteria."

We pulled on multiple layers of clothing for warmth and tromped through the snowy elements to the student center. Larry and his skinny, comical friend Kevin were waiting for us when we arrived, cafeteria trays tucked under their arms. After some quick introductions, we left, impatient for adventure. Large, lacey snowflakes continued falling as we chatted and hurriedly plowed through a foot of snow walking toward Pathfinder Hill, a steep road beside Burman Hall leading to a small creek. The chilly, frosty air was invigorating. It felt marvelous to be outside in the beautiful snowy landscape.

The flurries continued as we prepared to launch. Kevin was the first to fly down the snowy slope, and then Larry demonstrated how incredibly fun it was. Maria and I stood watching.

"I'm afraid we won't stop in time, and we'll end up on the bridge or in the creek," I said to Maria.

"Me, too," she replied. "They make it look so easy. They didn't land in the creek or on the bridge."

"No, they didn't, so we should be okay," I said, trying to convince myself that it really would be okay.

"What if someone sees us? We might get in trouble."

"Maybe," I said. "They wouldn't like to see us using cafeteria trays. But thankfully nobody is here."

When Larry returned to fetch one of us for a ride, I was the first candidate to climb on the improvised sled directly behind him. I was screaming all the way as we both sailed down the incline, the frozen icy snow gently pelting our faces. All too soon, our tray stopped at the base of the hill. We lingered for a few minutes, watching as the snowflakes landed.

"So, how was it?" Larry asked, gleaming with excitement as we climbed back up the hill.

My eyes were glistening, and a huge smile spread across my face. "I truly enjoyed it!" I quickly responded.

When it was Maria's turn to descend, I watched from the hilltop. She, too, was screeching on her first descent. At first, we sailed down with the guys, but as we became braver, we began going down the hill alone. It was practically dark, but a large lamppost and the moon and stars lit our way as we repeated the process of scrambling on and off the well-worn trays. Between the gorgeous scenery, our merriment, and the atmosphere of excitement, it was difficult to wait for another opportunity to soar down the hill.

As we headed up the hill toward our dorms that evening, we talked. "What will the cafeteria workers say about the trays?" I asked.

"They'd never imagine where the trays have been," Kevin replied laughing.

We all began laughing when he held up the trays. The bottoms were scratched and chipped.

"Look," he said pointing to his sled. "The corner has broken off from our adventures tonight."

"I think we should just store them in our rooms," Larry responded sheepishly. "It's too embarrassing to return them to the cafeteria in this condition."

Maria and I talked about how much fun we'd had as we headed to our dorm room. We concluded that they were fun and crazy guys. Larry seemed to be a pleasure seeker, always searching for something wild and daring to do. His adventurous spirit filled us with happiness and joy that night. Our feet were half frozen when we returned to our room, but our eyes sparkled with merriment.

A few weeks later, Larry called again. It was winter break, which was a four-day break that allowed students to leave campus and travel to Camp Au Sable for the weekend for a winter retreat. Although going home was an option, I'd chosen to stay at Andrews, and Larry had decided to remain behind as well. The frequency of his phone calls had increased, and as always, I was delighted that he'd phoned. I couldn't have asked for a better way for a friendship to develop.

"Am I bothering you?" he asked as he always did.

"No," I said. "Maria left for Camp Au Sable a few hours ago."

"Would you like to go sledding again?" he asked. "The snow is really coming down now. It's an ideal evening to go sledding!"

I didn't need much prodding.

"Sure," I said. "I'd love to!"

"Meet me at the student center in fifteen minutes," Larry said.

Tugging on my coat, hat, and gloves, I headed over to the student center, eager for another sledding adventure. It was indeed the perfect snowy evening for sledding. Enormous flakes descended, and the snow was already almost a foot deep. Light, feathery flakes transformed the campus, creating breathtaking grandeur. Larry and I journeyed by foot to Pathfinder Hill with our shabby cafeteria trays in hand. The flawless snow-white path was perfect for sledding. We took turns, joyfully flying down the hill as the swirling flurries pelted our faces. Larry, being the gentleman that he was, always waited at the bottom of the hill as I sailed down. Then he assisted me as we ascended the slippery snowy slope for another try. That glorious winter evening, patches of ice covered the majority of the ground, and we cruised much farther than we had before.

As we scrambled up the hilltop for the last time, Larry said, "I have homemade cookies in my dorm room. Would you like one?" he asked with a twinkle in his blue eyes.

"Sure! That would be fabulous!" I said, smiling back at him.

"Okay, wait here for just a minute," he said when we neared Meier Hall. "I'll go get them."

My face and lower extremities were thoroughly chilled when we ended our adventure that evening, but I patiently waited near the rear exit of his dorm. A few minutes later, he returned with two chocolate chip cookies in his hand. From there, we tromped back to the student center. Larry dropped off the well-worn trays in the student center. Nibbling our cookies, we meandered through campus, talking and enjoying the freedom from our studies. Larry took me into the science complex, a building I never frequented, and told me about his classes as we walked around. We talked for what seemed like hours before returning to our dorm rooms.

"Thank you for the cookies," I said with a smile as I walked through the door to my dorm hall. I couldn't stop thinking about how kindhearted and thoughtful he was. Memories of that splendid evening replayed in my dreams that night.

7

BURMAN HALL

Early one winter evening, I was interrupted from my studies by a loud knock on my dorm room door. Before I could open the door, Emilia barged in asking, "Would you like to go to Burman Hall for church on Sabbath? They have a special program that Larry and I want to go to."

"Sure," I said. "When does it start?"

"It begins at 10:30 on Sabbath morning, so meet me in my room at 10:15 and we'll walk over to Burman Hall and meet Larry there."

"Okay, sounds good," I replied.

On Sabbath morning, I put on one of my flowery Laura Ashley dresses and nylons and prepared for church. Then I headed over to Emilia's room so we could walk over to the church service together. It was cold, so we walked briskly during the five-minute trip to the men's dormitory. There was a bite to the air that cut through the multiple layers of clothing that we were wearing. No snow flurries were falling that day. Several feet of snow were piled in the grass beside the sidewalks, but thankfully the pathway to the men's dormitories were clear of snow. Soon, we arrived in the lobby of Burman Hall. Sun streamed through the many windows of the foyer, lighting up the room. Beautiful pictures hung on the walls, making the white paint come to life. Comfortable sofas and chairs were scattered tastefully throughout the room, and classical hymns were piping through the ceiling speakers. The air was filled with the chatter of many high-spirited, cheerful voices in the room.

Larry appeared in the lobby shortly after we entered. A smile crossed my face as my eyes met his. My cheeks flushed after a few moments, and shyness caused me to look away. I kept glancing back at him. There was a sparkle in his blue eyes. He looked especially handsome in his suit and tie. Emilia was her typical, talkative self. Her chatter broke the spell I felt when I saw Larry, and just as suddenly the timidity I'd felt dissipated. I was back in my friends' company, relaxed and ready for the service. Larry, forever the gentleman, led the way and escorted us to our seats. Larry sat to my left and Emilia to my right.

I don't remember much about the service now, except for the songs we sang. The one song that stands out in my mind was one I'd sung from the time I was a child, "Side by Side We Stand."[3] As the congregation sang, a large circle formed in the room as everybody joined hands. I nervously clasped Larry's hand when he offered it to me. Holding hands with Larry on my left and Emilia on my right, we sang:

> *Meet me in heaven*
> *We'll join hands together*
> *Meet me by the Savior's side*
> *I'll meet you in heaven*
> *We'll sing songs together*
> *Brothers and sisters, I'll be there*

I remember thinking how awesome it would be spending time in heaven with all my friends. Standing there between Larry and Emilia, I was thankful to have such amazing, caring people in my life. Later in the service, we were asked to hug the people next to us. I hugged Emilia. Then, as I turned to Larry, I found myself too embarrassed to hug him. Larry watched me, read my feelings, and knew how I felt. I could see that he wouldn't have minded hugging me, but he was thoughtful and made the choice to keep his distance and respect my needs. I was thankful. His behavior proved to me that he was more concerned about others than himself. It also showed me that he respected my boundaries when it came to touch. He held back when he knew I was uncomfortable. This told me that he was a true gentleman and that he was safe to be with. I knew that he would never hurt me or do something that I was uncomfortable with.

This was important to me as a relative had tried to defile me in the past. By the grace of God, I was spared from what could have been a terribly traumatic experience. I realized in that moment that Larry would never do anything to hurt me. This was an important concept for me to grasp. He respected me, and I knew he would never take advantage of me to gratify his own pleasures. In this day and age, men need to understand that touch is something very personal. Men often go for their own passion and violate women in the process. What men don't realize is that, while their bodies have external organs, women's organs are internal and extremely personal. Men can walk away from this event without as much devasting emotional damage and pain that this forced action causes women. I was thankful that Larry understood this. He accepted me as I was, shyness and all, and he respected my boundaries.

~8~

A SPRING WALK

Springtime always made me feel close to God. Weather warmed, and the snow finally melted. Birds were singing cheerfully one Sabbath afternoon when Larry called.

"Are you busy?" he asked.

"No," I said, waiting for him to share his reason for calling.

Larry was forever the one coming up with engaging activities. He was always eager for some new adventure. This day was no exception.

"Would you like to take a walk?" he asked.

"Sure!" I replied, envisioning his twinkling eyes. "I'll meet you in West Lobby in fifteen minutes," I said enthusiastically with a smile on my face, thrilled that he was planning and arranging activities for us. In the weeks since Larry's first phone call, he and I had become very good friends. We engaged in simple activities. After all, we were college students with little extra money. Our times together were filled with simple pleasures that didn't cost money but created lasting memories. This was one of those times. Larry loved nature as much as I did, and we had some wonderful times just enjoying each other's company and talking. Touch was not the foundation of our friendship; conversation was. This was the beauty of our relationship.

Larry was staring intently at me when I arrived in West Lobby. I caught his glance, and our eyes met for a few brief seconds. There was always an attraction between the two of us. He was my first serious friend who was a boy. I never really hung out with any guys when I was in elementary or high school, because I always felt uncomfortable and shy around them. But Larry was different. He and I connected on a deep level, and I felt completely at ease in his presence. I was always thrilled to spend time with him. There was a magnetic pull that drew the two of us together.

"Are you ready to go?" he asked with a huge boyish grin.

"Yes, I am," I said.

He tenderly glanced down at me as he held the door open. We exited the dorm and wandered outside. The sun shone radiantly, and the sky was a brilliant blue. Blooms and buds unfolded from fresh foliage, and it felt marvelous to be outdoors admiring the beauty without coats.

"Where should we go?" Larry asked glancing over at me.

"I really don't care. I'm just thankful to be outside," I said as we meandered through the campus and surrounding neighborhoods without a specific direction in mind.

Eventually, Larry asked, "Why not walk down into town?"

It would be a long walk, but both of us enjoyed the physical activity. As we passed through the neighborhoods, we talked.

"I can't wait until I have my own home," I said. "I'm looking forward to pruning the trees and shrubs. I love how nice, careful pruning makes the trees and bushes look." I stopped to point out an example. "I don't like the electric hedge cutters, because they don't make the shrubbery look as nice. When I have my own home, I'll prune everything by hand, the old-fashioned way, so everything looks nice."

"You must really enjoy gardening," Larry said with a smile, looking intently into my eyes.

"I do! Every summer I work in a perennial garden. I love caring for the flowers. It's such peaceful, relaxing work, being out in nature. I feel so close to God when I'm gardening."

"My dad enjoys gardening, too," Larry said. "Sometimes when we were kids, he'd have us help him. I never liked weeding though."

"I never liked weeding either when I was a kid, but now I do because I can see the progress and how much nicer things look."

As we walked into town, Larry developed an idea. His forever-curious mind was anxious to go exploring.

"Let's go see the dam," Larry said, his eyes gleaming at me with enthusiasm, making my heart skip a beat. "I often go down there with friends."

"I've never been there. You'll have to lead the way."

He patiently guided me down the path. "It's really not hard to find," he remarked. "We just head toward the bridge and then take the path that leads under it, which will take us right there." He guided me as he talked, walking just fast enough to ensure that I was close behind him. Periodically, he would turn around to make sure I was okay. When we finally arrived there, several fishermen were casting their lines under the bridge with the hope of catching something.

Only a few other people used the path that day, and as we approached the dam, we were again alone.

It was quiet except for the sounds of nature and our conversation. Larry's eyes glistened whenever I looked over at him. I couldn't help noticing the happiness and enthusiasm that I saw staring back at me. He always made me smile and laugh. There was so much enjoyment for life inside of him. His spontaneity and enthusiasm drew me out of my introverted world and made my heart happy.

Larry was forever curious and full of adventure, so when I saw interesting things, I would point them out to him. It was always exciting to see how he would react to these discoveries.

Suddenly, I saw something intriguing and I yelled to him, "Larry, look!"

A broad, vertical vine shaped like a swing hung from the newly green trees. It was curly and looked like something fun to explore. All I needed to do was call Larry's attention to something intriguing and sudden pleasure ensued.

Larry stood there for a few seconds looking at it and then he said, "Maybe we can swing on it." Suddenly, he was trotting over to it. "I'll climb up and see how well it works." I think he was hoping that it would allow both of us to swing on it, but his forever-caring side wanted to make sure it was safe first. Larry did manage to swing a bit, but the branches were flimsy and feeble, more so than he first thought. After a few minutes, he decided that it wasn't worth the risk and scrambled back down, and we resumed our walk toward the dam.

Arriving at the roaring dam, we stood watching the crashing water. The noise was earsplitting, which made it difficult for us to hear each other. Instead of lingering, we continued our walk so it was easier to talk. The day was winding down, and I had an idea. We had arrived at a familiar location, and I remembered the hours I'd spent there during my freshman year.

"Let's go to the park in Berrien. I'll show you where we did excavations during my freshman year as part of my archaeology class to determine whether or not it was a historical landmark."

"Where's that?" he asked. "I've never been there."

"I'll show you. We're very close to it. It's right next to the lake."

When we finally reached the park, we explored while I regaled him with stories about the unique items we had found during my freshman year.

"We found lots of clay pigeons here during our excavations," I said. "People use those for target shooting. We also discovered a bone!" Larry listened with intent curiosity.

Unwilling to break the magic developing between us, we slowly made our way back to Andrews. As we approached campus again, our conversation turned to the upcoming examinations and our vacation. In a couple of weeks, winter quarter would be over.

"What are you doing for spring break?" I asked.

"Oh, I'll be taking the train home," Larry said pensively. There were a few moments of silence, and I glanced over at him and noticed that he was deep in thought.

"I can't wait to see my horse," he said, but there was a bitter sweetness to his voice. "I love my horse. I'd love for you to meet my horse."

"I'd like that," I said grinning at him. My heart was racing inside of me.

"My horse is one of my favorite parts of being home." Then another silence followed as a somber expression spread across his face. In that quiet, I knew that Larry was thrilled to see his sister and family whom he loved so deeply, but I also sensed that he endured profound struggles and challenges in his home life. He seldom talked about this, but there was an undercurrent inside of him that was filled with pain from his past. I didn't press him about this in that voiceless moment. Finally, the silence was broken by a question.

"What are you doing for spring break?" he asked.

"I'll be heading home, too. It will be wonderful to see my family and cat again."

When we returned to campus, I felt refreshed and invigorated. I went back to my room with a huge smile on my face and happiness in my heart.

A few days later, my phone rang.

"Hello?" I said when I picked up the receiver.

"This is Larry. I hope I'm not bothering you."

"No, you aren't. My exams are over."

"Mine are, too," he said. "I called to let you know that I'm heading home. I just wanted to tell you goodbye. I'll see you when I get back."

"Bye," I replied. "Enjoy your break."

"You, too."

I sure would miss Larry.

~9~

A DINNER INVITATION

I had only been on campus for a couple hours after returning from my much-needed spring break when the ringing phone interrupted what I was doing.

"Hey," I heard when I picked up the receiver. "This is Larry. I'm at the train station. My roommate hasn't gotten back yet, and I'm stuck here. Would you mind coming to get me?" he asked with hesitation in his voice as if he didn't want to bother me.

"I'll come pick you up," I said, more than willing to help him. "Where are you?"

He gave me the directions. "I'll wait alongside the road for you."

"Okay, I'll be there soon."

I grabbed my keys and rushed out the door. It was only a ten-minute drive to the station. With my vacation over, thoughts about the approaching quarter consumed my mind as I drove. I knew that I'd be registering for exciting and challenging new classes, but I wasn't quite prepared to meet the stress and demands that the quarter would press upon me. When I arrived, Larry was waiting alongside the road with his assorted bags of luggage.

"Hi," I said to him when I arrived, noticing a little apprehension when he saw me. Looking back, I know now that this expression was because of a situation that had occurred with his dad over break; Larry loved him deeply, but their relationship wasn't without difficulties. Growing up sometimes presents its challenges as a person begins to stretch their wings and become independent. This appeared to be some of their struggle.

He calmed down a bit after unlocking my trunk to store his possessions. I caught his glance, and our eyes locked on each other briefly before we got in my car. As usual, Larry's tall frame hardly fit into my small red hatchback, but he climbed in without complaint. His eyes were still glued to my face. In the brief glances I made his way, I could tell he was relaxing and that he was thrilled to see me again.

"Have you eaten supper?"

"No," I said. "Not yet."

"Well," he briefly paused, a goofy grin spreading across his face, "how about if I pay for your supper in return for your willingness to pick me up?"

"You don't have to worry about paying me back," I said playfully, smiling with excitement coursing through my racing heart. "It's not that far to the train station, and I certainly wasn't going to leave you stranded." I was thankful to see him again. His eyes were glued to me as a pleading expression crossed over his face.

"Please?" he said with hands folded as if in prayer. I glanced over at him, and his determined eagerness at the proposal of paying for my supper won me over. I couldn't disappoint Larry like that.

"Okay," I said, smiling.

Larry was beaming at me. His eyes were glistening, and a joyful, merry grin hung on his face. "So, what do you want? Does pizza sound okay, or would you prefer something else?"

"No, pizza sounds fine."

"Let's order takeout," Larry suddenly exclaimed. An idea was flooding his mind and filling him with his typical excitement. "We can eat it at the student center."

"Okay," I replied as I drove towards the tiny chain of restaurants in town. After a few minutes, we arrived at the pizzeria and Larry ordered a medium pizza with peppers, mushrooms, and olives. We waited and chatted as the pleasant aroma of tomato sauce and Italian seasonings wafted from the kitchen. The smell made my stomach rumble and my mouth water. Soon, our food was ready, and we drove the short distance to Andrews.

The usually boisterous student center was quiet that evening, which was a pleasant surprise. Everyone else must have delayed their arrival until the final possible minute. I was delighted with the calm, relaxing atmosphere. It was peaceful. The movie *Bambi* was playing, and a couple other people were silently watching it.

"Vacation passed too quickly," I said to Larry as we sat down.

"Yeah, it did," he replied as he sat the pizza box on the table. "Shall we pray?" he asked, looking at me intently. He offered a quick prayer before opening the box. We each took a slice, enjoying the delectable flavors of each bite.

"I'm so pleased that this is our final quarter of the school year," I said.

"Yeah, it is nice. Summer vacation is just around the corner." A calm, pensive expression filled his face.

"It is, and I can't wait," I said. "It sure was nice to sleep in and relax over break. I'm not quite ready for classes to begin again."

Larry nodded in agreement, but I could tell that more than anything he was thrilled to be back on campus. We settled down on a bench and watched the movie while we ate.

"I bet college students from public universities wouldn't be as likely to watch an animated Disney movie," I said between bites. "They probably would entertain themselves with different activities, or at least a more sophisticated movie selection. Maybe that's the difference between private universities and public ones."

"Yeah, you're probably right," Larry replied.

We watched the movie and finished our pizza in companionable silence. Years later, one scene from the movie remains prominent in my mind. Two delightful birds are chasing each other, excited and infatuated with one another. When Bambi asks the wise old owl what is wrong with them, the owl says, "They are twitterpated." That's what Larry and I were that spring quarter: twitterpated. Though I was unwilling to admit it at the time.

10

SPRING FEVER

With spring came change. For one thing, Emilia finally acquired a roommate. Her first had relocated soon after moving in, so it was no wonder she'd visited our room so frequently during winter quarter. Chatting was as necessary to Emilia as eating and drinking. Her new Puerto Rican roommate, Isabel, had dark black hair and eyes and a gentle, sweet disposition. Their shared cultural backgrounds created a bond between them. Isabel soon became another member in our circle of friends.

The night before classes began, my friends and I chatted about our spring break adventures and discussed our upcoming classes.

"What are you taking this quarter?" I asked the group with curiosity, as we all had different majors and usually had unique course schedules.

"I'm taking statistics," Isabel said.

"I am, too," I replied. "When is your class?"

"Mine is at 1:30 in the afternoon," she said.

"We're in the same class," I exclaimed with excitement. "That's awesome! I'm not good with math. English is my strength. If I have any questions, will you help me?"

"Sure," Isabel replied patiently. "We can walk to class together, too, if you want," she said with a warm smile on her face.

"I'd like that," I said, smiling back.

On the first day of class, Isabel and I ambled into the large auditorium where our class was held and we took seats near the center of the room. To my surprise, Larry strolled in and took a front row seat. After sitting down, he turned around, noticed me and Isabel, and yelled hi as he waved to us. His eyes were locked on mine, and I read happiness in them. Daily, Larry made a point to wave to us in class. Seeing him was the highlight of my day.

Larry and Isabel had met before, as they both were physical therapy majors. Both of them had kind and caring hearts that made that career path a good fit. At home, Larry provided care to his mom who had multiple sclerosis. It was a job Larry loved and excelled at, so the field of physical therapy was the perfect fit for his compassionate, thoughtful heart.

That spring was incredibly challenging and exhausting. Looking back, I realize I didn't start on the right foot, which made the pressures and stress worse. During the initial week of the quarter, I didn't study as intensely as I should have. I had lost my motivation to study after my lazy spring break, and the warmth and brilliance of the sunlit spring weather didn't help either. I ached for the freedom to stroll outside in nature rather than remain cooped up inside. When the first week of the quarter ended, I felt like a caged animal straining to escape from confinement. One Friday morning, I headed over to what I thought was a necessary statistics class and silently sat down. The longer I remained, the more I ached to leave.

Shortly after my arrival, Larry entered the room. When he saw me, he plopped down in the seat beside me.

"What's going on?" he whispered.

"The professor is just answering some questions," I said. "I thought this was an important class, but it looks like it's only a question-and-answer session to help students with homework. I was just thinking about leaving when you came in."

We settled back to listen, but the first few assignments had been easy. Neither of us really had any questions.

"Would you like to go for a walk?" Larry whispered to me.

"Sure," I answered. "I'd much rather take a walk. It's a perfect day for one."

Larry and I left, agreeing to meet at Lamson Hall, and I hurried back to my room. Anxious for some physical activity after being cooped up all day, I didn't waste any time changing. Soon, I met Larry in the lobby.

"Do you have any place in particular you want to go?" he asked.

"No," I replied. "I just want to get outside and enjoy the beautiful day."

"Let's hike behind Pathfinder Hill," he suggested. "I discovered some really cool trails back there recently."

"That sounds like a fabulous plan! It's been months since I've been back there in the woods."

We ambled along the paths, pointing out things that caught our attention. Suddenly, I spotted something I'd seen before.

"See that?" I pointed. "When I was a freshman, my friends and I spent Sabbath afternoons digging in junk piles back here. People have thrown out all kinds of things. You'd be amazed by what we've found buried in there."

For a few minutes, we looked through the junk pile, finding everything from glass jars to wheels and broken doors to windows. Larry stumbled upon something and called out. I joined him in investigating a crater in the ground.

"What kind of animal would have hollowed out such a gigantic hole?" I asked.

"I don't know," Larry replied, bending down to examine the opening.

Goose bumps rose on my arms, and the desire to scream escalated as I envisioned a wiggly, slimy snake emerging from the crevice.

"Maybe we should move on, Larry. Who knows what will come flying out of that cavity." I walked on purposefully to furnish Larry with an additional hint to stop his investigation of the hole. "Let's go explore something else. I'm not anxious to discover what type of animal has dug that hole," I said over my shoulder as I walked away, chewing on my lip. "I can just see something like a snake or some other creature scramble out of it."

Larry got the hint and sprinted after me. He was never one to tease me. His heart was too caring and thoughtful to do that. He took my hint and followed me, but it wasn't long until our pace slowed again as

Larry, always adventurous and inquisitive, spied a wooden structure.

"Someone built an Indian tepee," he said. "Let's check it out."

Larry was entertained by everything. We moved closer to examine the meticulous design, both of us admiring its construction and amazed at the creativity of its designers. The logs were woven together and fit into notches, just like a log cabin. We moved on and strolled past the school's dairy farm, back toward the college campus.

When I returned to my dorm a few hours later, invigorated by our excursion, it was almost sundown. Any productive studying was out of the question. I'd just have to wait until Sunday to accomplish everything else. Hurriedly, I cleaned my room and ate supper by myself. Maria and Emilia were gone for the weekend, so afterwards I opted to take a short nap.

I woke up around 6:30 PM and thought briefly about going to vespers, an evening prayer service. I was simply too sleepy, so instead I just lounged on my bed. The phone rang at about 7:30.

I answered it quickly, hoping it was Larry.

"Hi," Larry said. "Are you going to vespers tonight?"

"No," I yawned.

"I'm not very interested in going either," he said, and time sped by as we chatted. We could talk about anything. I don't think there was a topic we didn't discuss. Before we knew it, it was 11 PM. Neither of us could believe how quickly the time had passed.

"Which church are you going to tomorrow?" he asked before we hung up.

"Maria isn't here this weekend, so I'm planning on going to Pioneer Memorial."

"Would you like to go with me?" Larry asked.

"Sure," I said happily, looking forward to spending more time with him.

11

LARRY'S OFFER

Ass the quarter progressed, I started attending church with Larry on a more regular basis, and sometimes he frequented Spanish church with me, Maria, and Emilia.

One Sabbath morning, the phone rang.

"Hi, Debbie. This is Larry. Emilia agreed to attend the Seminary Sabbath School class with me, but I can't reach her. Can you check if she's in her room?"

I went next door and knocked, but nobody answered.

"I'm sorry. She's not in her room," I told him. "She must have left already. Maria and I are planning on going to Lamson Chapel for church. Would you like to meet us there? We'll be heading down in fifteen minutes."

"Sure! That's fine. I'll see you in a few minutes," he said.

We met Larry in the chapel. Shortly afterwards, Emilia joined us, and the four of us found seats. Emilia sat on my right side, and Larry on my left side. As the lengthy sermon continued, I became more and more antsy, wiggly, and fidgety after being cooped up all week. To calm myself, I began doodling on my church bulletin, attempting to draw roses.

When he noticed my roses, Larry whispered, "Those look wonderful! They sure look better than what I can do."

"Thanks," I said softly as I continued to draw. "I don't think they look that good, but it's fun to try."

As the quarter progressed, the frequency of Larry's phone calls increased and so did the duration of our conversations. On weekends, we chatted for hours. The time flew by when we talked. Gradually, a daily school routine also developed. Every day, Isabel and I headed off to statistics class together. At the conclusion of class, Larry scampered after us to chat with me. Even though it wasn't a long conversation, it was often the highlight of my day, a sparkling shiny focal point of the most stressful quarter of that year. The excitement and enthusiasm in Larry's voice always lightened my stress. I was constantly exhausted that quarter, but then who wouldn't be after averaging only four hours of sleep per night? That was the way the entire quarter proceeded, too. I didn't think I'd ever make it. Every time I'd snatch some sleep, the phone rang or a deafening knock resounded on my door, disturbing my sleep. Larry, as always, was sensitive and sympathetic about my utter fatigue that quarter. When he phoned, he always asked if he had awakened me. He was very aware that I was exhausted because I was constantly yawning, and often during conversations my eyelids would flutter shut. "You need some sleep," he'd say glancing at me as I battled yet again to keep my eyes open.

I was tremendously thankful for Larry that quarter. When I entered statistics class each day, I searched for his cheerful wave and handsome smile and looked forward to our conversations after class. These things refreshed me. I appreciated his enthusiasm, humor, and concern. He was the person who kept me glued together that quarter. Exercise, my typical sanity saver, was incredibly tricky to fit into my schedule. When I told Isabel about my exercise challenge, she told me that she was enrolled in a physical education class in which she was required to exercise every day. We resolved to go jogging together. That commitment provided the necessary incentive to rearrange my schedule to fit exercising into it. As the quarter progressed, our schedules changed, but at least Isabel provided the initial incentive to exercise again. I made it a habit to jog every day after statistics class.

One day after class, Larry joined us to chat. "What are your plans for this afternoon?"

"I'm changing clothes so I can go out and run," I said glancing into his blue eyes.

"Can I come along?" he asked with pleading eyes.

"Sure, meet me at East Lobby in ten minutes," I said as I raced off to my room.

I changed quickly, anxious to relieve the pent-up frustrations and worries of the day. I arrived at East Lobby shortly before Larry and patiently waited. When his familiar, preppy figure swiftly rounded the corner, I sprinted over to meet him. My excitement waned, though, when I saw he hadn't changed.

"I'm sorry," he said when he saw my downcast expression. "I can't go. When I went back to my room, I remembered I have an appointment this afternoon. I can't go."

"Okay," I said, trying to hide my disappointment. "I'll see you later. Have a good afternoon."

I was certain there was another reason behind his refusal. Something about his demeanor and expression told me that he was making excuses. Maybe he's like Emilia and doesn't enjoy jogging, I thought. Or maybe he's worried he can't keep up with me because he hasn't been exercising. My heart told me that he was afraid to go jogging, because he thought he wouldn't be able to keep up with me. My heart was heavy, and my happiness deflated. All that remained was disappointment. I presented my discontent to God as I ran. While I ran, my gloomy heart mellowed as I prayed. Peace replaced my sadness, and I finished my run more content than when I started it, even though Larry hadn't joined me.

12

THE 5K RACE

One Friday afternoon in mid-spring, a poster appeared in Lamson Hall announcing that a 5k race would be held in a few days. I grabbed a brochure and read the details. As soon as I returned to my room, I filled out the application. When I showed the brochure to Emilia and Maria a few days prior to the race, they thought it was an outstanding idea, especially since I exercised so faithfully. They felt certain I could do it, but neither of them were interested in joining me. Emilia suggested that instead I ask Sophie, a friend from her biology class. Sophie sometimes ran, too, and was earnestly considering running the race.

I'm not sure why Larry was not part of the race, and I don't remember why no one asked him to join in watching the event, but for some reason, he was out of the loop and unaware of our plans. Emilia was usually eager and ready to share any detail she could about what was happening in Lamson Hall, but she hadn't told him either. Whatever the case, even with all the commotion of people running around Meier and Burman Halls, Larry remained unaware of our participation.

The day of the race arrived, and the hustle and bustle of activity and excitement filled the air. Friday afternoon after statistics, I departed for my usual jog. As I ran, everyone was preparing for the alumni parade that began in an hour. The day was exceptionally humid, and by the time I returned to my room, I was wringing wet. When I arrived, Sophie was coaxing Emilia to join her in a jog, but Emilia stubbornly refused. Pleading, imploring, and beseeching were ineffective; she was immovable, and Sophie's requests fell on deaf ears.

Suddenly, Emilia noticed me entering the room. "Why don't you go running with Debbie?" she said pointing to me with obvious relief.

Observing my sweaty body and ruddy face, Sophie hesitantly asked, "Would you mind running again with me?"

"I think I can handle one more lap," I said.

Since she and I both needed to figure out our pace for the race on Sunday, that's what we did. By the time we returned, I'd totally and utterly burned up all my excess energy. Thankfully, it was Friday afternoon, so I could rest and relax until the race on Sunday.

The morning of the race, I awoke to brilliantly light blue skies and sunshine. A gentle breeze wafted through the trees. Although a chill was in the air, the radiant gleaming sun promised warmer temperatures, and I was glad that the race would occur in the morning before the heat soared. Sophie and I had planned on meeting around nine o'clock that morning. By the time I found her, she'd already signed up for the race and received her number. We darted to the parking lot in front of the administration building so I could register.

The crowds formed. Soon, a shout sounded over the noise of the crowd. "The 5k race is beginning. Please assemble on the starting line."

I nervously located a place on the starting line with Sophie and anxiously waited for the race to begin. Finally, the alarm sounded, and the race began. Sophie shot off in front of me when she heard the signal, but I knew my limitations. A few paces faster than normal were all I could achieve, or my asthma would flare up. Inhaler in hand, I watched Sophie dash past me. The shouting crowds energized me, and I sprinted a great deal faster than usual. Reaching the administration building my first time around the course, I saw Emilia cheering me on. She provided me with a much-needed boost to keep going. By the second circuit of the course, I was fatigued, but I was also determined to finish and pleased my asthma wasn't acting up. Knowing I was jogging my final lap, I headed towards Meier and Burman Halls, and I observed several people ahead. Determination to pass them gave me the will to make it through the short distance remaining. Finally, I saw the science complex and picked up my speed. I jogged as fast as I could, passing a couple more people. The magnificent finish line was finally in sight, only a few yards ahead with Emilia standing there cheering me on, camera in hand, ready to snap a picture as I crossed the finish line.

I made it. The race was over. Sophie stood at the finish line, encouraging me when I rushed by. I was totally exhausted but so pleased to have finished. Sophie and Emilia strolled around while I grabbed a cool drink at the refreshment table. Then Emilia motioned for Sophie and me to stand together so she could snap our picture. We waited for the awards to be announced, and when the winners were called Sophie's name was read. She had received a medal! The winners gathered for a picture. Sophie's happy, glowing face and that glorious snapshot will forever remain etched in my mind.

Later that afternoon, I received a phone call from Larry.

"Emilia told me you ran in the 5k race. Why didn't you tell me that you were running in it? I would have come if I'd known you were running it. I would have enjoyed cheering for you at the finish line."

I could envision the intense disappointment in his blue eyes, and through the phone I could hear his silent moaning.

"I'm so sorry," I said. "I would have enjoyed having you there! I thought Emilia mentioned it to you. It was something I decided to do at the last minute, and I guess in all the excitement, I didn't think about telling you."

"Next time I will be there," Larry vowed.

And I knew he would keep his promise.

~13~

ENGLISH COMPETITION

As the quarter progressed, I realized that Larry didn't appear to study much, and I wondered how he ever managed to pass any of his classes. Somehow, he seemed to breeze through even his harder subjects, such as chemistry or microbiology, with at least passing grades. I didn't understand how he managed. He must have simply retained information better than I did. I would've failed for sure if I studied like he did. While I spent most of my time holed up in my room studying, he found plenty of time for pleasure, amusement, and socializing. Just like Emilia, he loved being with people and had no difficulty talking to new acquaintances. He thrived on being around people, and everyone appreciated him. He knew all the students on campus, and everyone knew him.

Larry called Emilia frequently, and they were becoming excellent friends. Both of them were enrolled in freshman English. While Emilia relished the teacher of that class (probably because he continually presented her with excellent grades), Larry grew frustrated with the professor. The two of them were intensely competitive in that class. Larry was forever attempting to earn A's on his papers, but he struggled to turn his assignments in on time, which automatically reduced his grade. Emilia always gloated about the A's she received on her English papers.

"Guess what happened in English class today," she'd say grinning and laughing. Then she would proceed to inform me about the grade Larry received on his paper and how she was doing better in the class than he was.

"You shouldn't laugh at him like that," I'd protest. Just because she could whip out a paper in two hours and still get an A didn't mean everyone else could. I certainly couldn't. "Don't put him down."

Occasionally, other peers made fun of him although he always handled it good-naturedly, but knowing that those things hurt, I didn't think Emilia needed to add to it. However, I also intuitively knew that most of their competition arose out of good fun, and I'm certain she gloated more to me than to him. It gave her something to tease him about, and it did result in Larry studying harder in English. Maybe it was the incentive he needed to succeed so he could be accepted into the physical therapy program.

Occasionally, when Emilia was in my room, she would answer the phone when Larry called. I could hear his voice through the phone asking, "Is Debbie there?"

"You have the wrong room," she'd tease. "Dial the number again."

Sometimes I'd get upset with her, especially when she'd suddenly barge into my room while I was conversing with Larry. Her comments frequently distracted or embarrassed me.

"¡Cállate!" I'd frequently shout, attempting to convince her to be quiet.

Larry became extremely familiar with that word, since I used it so frequently. Sometimes I had to forcefully propel Emilia out the door and lock the door behind her. Larry always laughed when I finally resorted to this tactic. He thought it was humorous, even though he agreed it probably was the best way to ban her from bothering me.

When Larry called Emilia to see if she wanted to do something with him, she would frequently respond, "Why don't you call Debbie and ask her? I'm sure she would like to."

She would turn to me and say, "You need to go out and do more things."

And she was right on both counts. As the quarter progressed, her suggestions became more frequent, and I suspected it was a ploy to help me do something other than studying. She thought I was a hermit. Secretly, I'm certain she was playing matchmaker and brewing up ways to get me and Larry together. Whatever the case, she knew I admired Larry even though I never once said so. It was something that she simply sensed.

At the time, I wasn't entirely ready to admit to anyone how intensely and passionately I was growing to admire Larry. Friendship was extremely safe territory. I required certainty that the relationship had a solid foundation and could endure time before allowing my heartstrings to be bound. Friendship was the basis of any relationship, and I didn't want anything to destroy ours. Dating sometimes tore friendships apart, and I admired Larry too much to allow that to happen. Instead, I chose to take things slowly, something I suspect that Larry had difficulty understanding but he patiently acquiesced to my decision.

Something else also deterred me.

Larry was two and a half years younger than me. Although he seemed mature in some areas, in other areas his deep insecurities showed, and it was clear that he struggled to accept himself. Occasionally, he'd do silly immature things when he became embarrassed or self-conscious. I wasn't the only one who noticed this, and when others observed this, they teased him. One incident in particular is firmly etched in my mind. Larry and I were sitting with friends in the cafeteria, and everyone was busy eating and talking. After finishing his food, Larry became antsy and began playing with the items on his tray. Then he decided to construct a geometrical design with the assortment of items available. It didn't bother me. He was quietly occupied, but everyone else made a tremendous deal about it and teased Larry.

"Didn't you guys ever do this in high school?" Larry retorted.

Everybody shook their heads.

I said nothing, just quietly observed, frustrated and upset by their callous, insensitive comments. It didn't bother me in the least that Larry constructed an elaborate design on his tray; he was simply being creative and keeping himself busy as everyone else talked. Because I considered our friends' words out of line and immature, I attempted to steer the conversation in a different direction.

Larry goofed around at other times, too. Maybe it was because of nervousness or hyperactivity. Usually, it was fidgeting or fooling around with objects or his hands or pacing the room, but sometimes this activity made me uncomfortable. However, I tried to overlook my discomfort, because I believed I saw someone who felt insecure. There was a deep hurt inside of him, and instinctively I knew he'd suffered some harsh pain in his life, though he seldom discussed this with me.

Rather than focusing too much on his insecurities, though, my primary focus was on the aspects of his personality that I admired. He was charming and so compassionate and outgoing. His creativity in finding activities in the spur of the moment made me smile, and I valued his enthusiasm for life. I also admired his phlegmatic disposition. It mellowed me out. I was extremely driven and constantly worried about things. When I was tense and uptight, he never got upset. He simply listened and gently calmed me down. Larry helped me survive that quarter and the others that followed.

PICTIONARY

One Saturday evening, my friends and I met in my room to determine what we wanted to do that night. We discussed numerous options before Maria and I decided to peruse a selection of East Lobby board games to play. Bea, a music major, and her sister Sara were in East Lobby when we arrived, so we invited them to join us.

Pictionary looked fun, so we checked it out and headed over to Meier Hall. Then we called Larry, who invited a few others to join us in the lobby. Larry introduced us to the friends he'd brought: Kevin, Dan, and Peter, his roommate.

"We brought Pictionary," Maria said after our introductions. She handed the game to Larry.

"Okay, that sounds like fun," Larry replied. Then he motioned to some other guys in the lobby. "Would you like to join us? We're going to play Pictionary."

We sat down, and the other guys, Caleb and Paul, who were also in the lobby joined us. Kevin, the group comedian, began cracking jokes, and we laughed.

"Let's divide into groups and play a round," Larry finally said gesturing to all of us.

So, we split up into teams, and Larry, as usual, joined mine. We were in a group with Bea, Sara, and Paul. Caleb, Kevin, Peter, Dan, and Maria were in the other group.

Despite what Larry thought about my doodling on Sabbath bulletins, I wasn't completely confident in my drawing abilities, so before the game started, I suggested that we allow people to act out words if they wanted instead of drawing them. Thankfully, everyone else agreed to the option of charades.

Pictionary requires split-second decisions, which can either add to the fun of the game or can lead to embarrassment. Towards the end of the evening, Larry drew a card and stood thinking intently for a few seconds as he decided how to convey it to us. I was sitting to the right of Larry, and Bea was on his left. In retrospect, it should have been easy to guess, but for some reason our team was having a hard time. Initially, he started pursing his lips and blowing air into the sky. When none of us guessed the word, he pursed his lips and put them on his hand. We still were at a loss. Frustrated, Larry momentarily paused, thinking carefully about the next best way to act out the word. He knew there was one sure way to convey the word. He glanced briefly and longingly at me, and then turned and puckered his lips on Paul's cheek! Of course, we all guessed the word then. "Kiss!" we all shouted. Everyone, that is, except Paul, who wasn't too happy about the fact that Larry had kissed him. We all broke out in gales of laughter.

A mortified expression crossed Paul's face as he wiped off his cheek. "Why didn't you kiss one of the girls?" he asked, obviously horrified as he pointed to me, Bea, and Sara. "Why did you have to kiss me?"

Then I knew what Larry's brief glance at me had meant. He had wanted to kiss me, but in order to save me from embarrassment, he had refrained.

Paul's disgruntled response resulted in raucous laughter. After everything calmed down, I felt badly that Larry was teased so much, but I hadn't been any better since I'd contributed by laughing, too. Being a gracious person, though, Larry had taken it all in stride.

~15~

A WILLING SUBJECT

That spring, I was enrolled in an introductory audiology course for which I was required to practice performing hearing evaluations. Unfortunately, stumbling upon eager individuals wasn't easy. Everyone was incredibly busy. Maria wasn't willing to undergo testing, so instead I hunted for other subjects. By the middle of the quarter, I was growing desperate.

"Emilia," I coaxed. "Please, could I do a hearing evaluation on you this Sunday?"

"No!" she said, digging in her heels at the thought. "I'll be gone this weekend, anyway. Why don't you ask Larry? I'm sure he'd be willing to help you out. I'll talk to him."

When Larry heard of my need, he agreed to be my guinea pig. I was thankful he was willing to help. The assignment was due in two days, and I would not have time to perform it later that week. So, on Sunday afternoon, Larry and I agreed to meet at the speech and hearing department. Overcast skies greeted me that day, and showers poured from above. It was one of those gray, dismal days when the sun was hidden with little hope of its brilliant appearance. I raced over to my department, umbrella in hand. Since Larry wasn't there when I arrived, I chatted with the students who were there. A classmate was conducting a hearing evaluation when I entered, so I waited. The student's session was still in progress when Larry popped in a few minutes later.

"Someone is still testing," I said. "I can't test you for at least another half hour. Is that okay?" We chatted for a bit, but I could tell that Larry was uncomfortable waiting in the lobby of my department.

Finally, I said, "Can you meet me here in about twenty-five minutes?"

"Sure," he said. "I'll see you then."

When Larry returned, the audiometer—the machine utilized to conduct hearing tests—was free. We entered the sound booth, and after he was as comfortable as he could be, I proceeded to provide Larry with instructions.

"I have to place these headphones on you," I said as I positioned them on his ears. "Please raise your hand when you hear the noises."

Because I was inexperienced, I was incredibly slow at figuring out the testing procedures. There were oodles of steps to move through as I manipulated the dials on the audiometer to determine his hearing thresholds. First, there were dials that had to be turned to establish the frequency ranges in both ears and buttons that had to be pushed to move up and down on the loudness levels of the sounds to determine the hearing thresholds. There were several frequency ranges to test. I had to move through each frequency range to find the loudness level at which he was hearing. I struggled to review my notes and remember the information I'd learned in class as I plotted his hearing on my audiogram, the graph showing the hearing thresholds. I had to carefully ensure that I was performing the test correctly. Thankfully, Larry was patient and didn't complain for the entire hour of testing. He was the perfect subject, and I was incredibly appreciative.

Once the lengthy ordeal was over, we were both relieved to be free from the stuffy confines of the sound booth. It was supper time. Larry and I braved the dreary weather on our way to the noisy cafeteria, where we found our friends in the packed dining area.

Maria, however, arrived after Larry and I had started eating. She'd just completed a Mary Kay facial, and she waltzed into the room with an enormous smile on her face, her excitement and enthusiasm about the products evident. She described her afternoon and how the Mary Kay consultant had asked her to be the model, and had used Maria to demonstrate how to apply the makeup. None of us were accustomed to seeing Maria with makeup, since she normally didn't wear any. It took time to adjust to the difference.

"What do you think?" Maria asked. "Do you think it looks all right?"

Everyone was quiet for a moment. Larry was first to comment.

"I think it's a little much," he said gently.

Her face fell. "Someone told me that I look like a clown."

"The color is nice," I said. "It just needs to be brushed out so it looks more natural. That would tone the color down. Then you'd be fine."

When Maria disappeared to purchase her food, Larry leaned over and whispered in my ear, "I think she's wearing too much makeup."

"Yes, probably so," I said, reluctant to criticize but wanting to be truthful. "But if she brushed it out, it would tone down the colors. You just have to work with it to make it look good."

Larry was quiet for a moment. Then he said, "Maybe so, but I like a more natural look. I like the way you apply your makeup."

I felt a thrill shoot through me as I realized that Larry admired the naturalness of my appearance.

~16~

ROOMMATE PROBLEMS

As rough as that quarter was for me, I have many pleasant memories of that time. Larry's frequent phone calls alleviated my stress and maintained my sanity. One Sunday afternoon, I'd been diligently studying for almost two hours when the phone rang.

"Would you like to go for a walk?" Larry asked.

"Sure," I said eagerly. "That sounds wonderful!"

Larry must have sensed my anxiety about the extreme piles of homework. "It'll be a short one," he said.

"That sounds good," I replied with relief, both at the break and the reassurance that I could resume my studies shortly.

We met at East Lobby and began ambling around campus.

"How are things going for you and Maria?" he asked.

"Fine."

He was quiet for a moment, then he said, "Peter—you know, my roommate—and I aren't getting along very well." I could hear a somber, serious tone to Larry's normally exuberant voice. The typical sparkle and gleam were missing in his eyes.

"I can feel the tension mounting between us," Larry continued, "but I don't know what to do. Sometimes Peter stays up late playing computer games when I want to go to bed and keeps me awake asking me questions about how to play the game. But then when I play computer games, it distracts Peter when he's trying to study." I didn't say anything, but I felt myself frowning. It was a vicious cycle for the two of them.

"I end up staying up late at night because Peter keeps me awake, and then I have to get up early in the morning to get ready for my seven o'clock class. It's getting more difficult for me to wake up in the morning when my alarm goes off. Sometimes I don't even hear my alarm. Peter has a later morning class so he can sleep in, and it makes me mad that he gets to sleep in. If I could get to bed earlier, maybe I could get up when my alarm goes off in the morning."

"It can be challenging to room with someone, especially with the small confines of a dorm room," I said, trying to both respect him and to be diplomatic. "There's no privacy. Maria and I also struggle with our sleeping schedules. It's so easy to wake somebody up without meaning to because of the tiny space of the dorm rooms. I'm sure I get on her nerves sometimes, too. In spite of our frustrations, we try to be considerate of each other."

There was extreme sorrow and pain on Larry's face. His normally relaxed, optimistic attitude was replaced with stress and frustration. I ached for his optimistic outlook on life to return. I needed to encourage and help him. Pausing for a moment before continuing, I silently prayed the Lord would provide me with words of encouragement and wisdom.

"Sometimes Maria's talking on the phone can be annoying, especially when I'm trying to sleep, but I've learned to ask her to go outside and talk on the phone. The close quarters in the dorms make it difficult, though. The school year is almost over," I said, endeavoring to encourage Larry. "You can choose a different roommate next year."

He felt slightly better when he thought about that Not many more weeks remained. His mood lifted as we finished our walk, the time slipping rapidly away.

~17~

A FAILED EXAM

As was typical for that stressful quarter, I had three exams scheduled in one day and knew that in order to survive I'd have to prepare ahead of time. There was no way I could study for all three exams in one evening. I didn't know how I'd ever manage to pass all those tests. I studied arduously, prayed fervently, and cancelled my work for that week.

Finally, the stressful test day arrived. I finished my first test and hurried back to my room to review my notes for the second one. In just a few minutes I'd be taking my next test. As I was sitting at my desk studying, the phone rang. It was my mom. For weeks she'd been talking about coming up to visit her sister who lived in the area. Her hope was to make the trip when I was at Andrews so she could visit with me as well. I was looking forward to seeing her again and had been impatiently anticipating her visit all quarter. She called to tell me she couldn't visit that weekend because she was having some challenges at work.

Boy, she sure picked an excellent time to tell me, I thought as I hung up the phone. Although I knew that her job was stressful and busy, I was disappointed she couldn't visit. I wasn't certain that I'd be able to concentrate on my next test after that news, but somehow, I managed. Statistics, though, was another story. The moment I received my test, everything I had learned vanished from my mind. I couldn't remember anything. Beads of sweat streamed down my forehead as I leafed through the exam, searching for problems I understood. My heart sank and my stomach tightened. It was hopeless. Even my prayers seemed to be unheard. I somehow managed to answer most of the problems, but as I left the room, I knew I'd failed. I didn't want to see my grade.

I ran back to my room, stretched out on my bed, and sobbed, praying that the Lord would comfort me. I couldn't even bring myself to go running; I'd have to jog off my frustration later. As I lay there in a heap on my bed, weeping uncontrollably, the phone rang. Depressed and gloomy, I ignored it a few more times before I hauled myself over to answer it, wishing for time to regain my composure. When I answered the phone, Larry's cheerful voice sounded from the other end.

"How'd you do?"

"Not very well," I managed to say. "I failed that exam."

"I don't think I did very well either," he said. "But you always study a lot, so you probably did better than you think. You usually do fine."

"No," I said. "I completely blanked out. I couldn't remember anything. I know I failed it. Normally, during a math test I don't feel like I have enough time, but this was different, Larry, I just sat there guessing at the answers."

He tried his best to comfort me, and his words did help. By the end of the conversation, I was feeling better, and I had enough energy to go for the intense jog I needed to burn off the remainder of my frustration.

18

A SIMPLE PRAYER

The summer did not gradually arrive as it normally did. The weather went from cold to extremely hot and humid almost overnight. It was unbearable. To make matters worse, the air-conditioning wasn't working anywhere on campus except the girls' dormitory. Unfortunately for me, my room was in the older wing of the dormitory, the side that didn't have any air-conditioning. It felt like a sauna, and I was sweltering and sweating so profusely that I was finding it almost impossible to study.

The phone rang one blisteringly hot afternoon. I heard Larry's usual optimistic voice on the other end.

"How are you doing?" he asked.

"I'm sweltering," I said miserably, yet grateful to hear his voice.

"I thought the air-conditioning was working at the girl's dormitory," he said.

"It is, but I'm living in the old wing, and there is no air-conditioning in this section, so it's extremely hot. It's just like a sauna."

"Our air-conditioning isn't working in Meier Hall either, so it's incredibly hot here, too."

"I'm praying the weather will cool down for exam week. I can't concentrate in conditions like this," I said.

"That would be wonderful." Larry answered. "I could handle some cooler weather as well."

Larry called again later that week. He asked if I would go with him to the spring banquet that the student association was sponsoring. I said I would. I was thrilled about his offer and excitedly told Maria about it when she entered the room. As the week passed though, I began to seriously question the wisdom of going. I knew Larry liked me, and I was growing fonder of him with each passing day. Yet something powerful restrained me. It was as if the reins of my halter were being tugged viciously to drag me to a sudden stop. Was it God or my fears?

I truly admired Larry and delighted in his friendship, but I simply wasn't ready for a romantic relationship. The formal setting of a banquet frightened me. I didn't want anything to jeopardize or destroy the friendship we had. Because of numerous divorces in my family and my own parents' divorce, I've always had tremendous shyness and caution with men. My desire was to break this chain in our family history. I needed God to lead and direct me. It was His assurance and peace that I needed, so I prayed fervently for God's wisdom.

A few days later, I shared with my friend Robin that Larry had invited me to the banquet. She was surprised by the news and voiced concerns about Larry being immature. She suggested I date Evan, because he was more mature. Maybe God was enlightening me about something. All I knew was that I didn't want to engage in a romantic dating relationship yet. We both needed time to mature, and I needed undeniable certainty that Larry was indeed God's plan for my life.

My biological father's abandonment and my stepfather's disconnectedness had made a permanent impact on me. I had so little modeling of what a true father should be like. This affected my relationship with men. For years, I had struggled with boys, until Larry came along. Larry was the first man that I'd admired so deeply, my first true friend who was a boy. He was like a breath of fresh air to me, and for the first time I was comfortable with a male. He felt like an old friend or a comfortable pair of jeans. But I also could see deeply inside of Larry, and I knew that he, too, had come from a dysfunctional home. He struggled with hurt and pain just as I did. I was so confused about what I should do. I enjoyed talking to Larry, and we had so much fun together. But I was not ready for him to be my boyfriend.

When Robin came along, her concerns illuminated the insecurities inside of me. It tied me into knots and consumed me with fear. These were things that fed into my internal turmoil and filled me with overwhelming feelings of confusion. Questions plagued my mind. Why couldn't I push past all of this and focus on the good things? Larry cared, he was thoughtful, he respected my boundaries, he was patient, he was gentle... He had so many good characteristics. But, once concerns were voiced, it was all my mind could focus on. The fear tied a noose so firmly around me that it almost strangled me. I prayed, but even after prayer I was a mess emotionally. All I needed was just a little space, a break to sort out my thoughts. I phoned Larry and informed him that I couldn't go to the banquet. For Larry, I could see that my decision was a hard blow. His studies plummeted, and I felt horrible and rotten about that. After all he'd done, how could I have been so heartless and mean? Even now, I can't believe how messed up my thoughts were then. He was so perfect for me. Why was I so confused?

Forever patient, Larry gave me the space I needed even though it hurt him deeply. He gave me time to sort out my thoughts and to settle my fears. He didn't press me or call me. Instead, he gave me the gift of time. In my prayers, I asked God to show me whether Larry was right for me. *Lord, you know that the enormous number of divorces in my family causes me to be cautious. Please show me if Larry is the person you want me to date. Please critique the men I've become acquainted with this year and remove the men you don't want me to date.* After that prayer, I felt at peace knowing that God would continue to direct my path. God had the perfect plan for my life. I knew I could trust Him. Larry and I didn't communicate much during the last few weeks of that quarter, and I noticed he wasn't attending statistics class. I hoped it wasn't because of me, but something told me that it was. My life was so busy that I didn't have much time to think about it. The pressures of the quarter were paying a toll on me. Exhaustion consumed me. The days of the quarter were passing quickly, and summer was around the corner. The last weeks of school were hectic, and the extreme humidity and temperatures made it miserable. Everyone was suffering. As I studied, I could feel beads of perspiration dripping down my back. When the weather continued to remain hot and humid, the majority of the women in the dorm evacuated the stuffy confines of the sauna. We piled into the air-conditioned lobbies, and I prayed the scorching weather would subside. Gratefully, the Lord heard my prayers. Dark, ominous rain clouds approached, and the temperatures cooled considerably. All of us were relieved for the cooler weather.

I still hadn't heard from Larry, but he continued to be in my thoughts and prayers. I knew that it was almost his birthday, so I asked my friends if they'd like to help me plan a birthday party for him. They thought it was a great idea. Emilia volunteered to bring the cups and plates, Isabel would supply drinks, and I would bring the cake. I called Larry and invited him to East Lobby for vespers that Friday evening. He happily accepted the invitation without questioning my motive. My friends and I prepared food for his party and carried it all down to the lobby. Larry was anxiously waiting when we entered. We sang "Happy Birthday" to him. His face showed a surprised expression and his normally talkative self was silent for a few moments as we sliced the cake and served the food.

"Thank you!" Larry said, eyes beaming and face glowing as he unwrapped presents.

Then we chatted. It was wonderful talking to everyone, but I noticed that Larry had his eyes on his watch. He was uncomfortable and unusually quiet. About an hour later, everyone started leaving.

Larry stood abruptly and told us he had to go. He seemed sullen and depressed that evening. Something was bothering him. I hadn't spoken to him much in the last couple weeks. Worried about Larry, I called to check on him later that night. When I phoned, his roommate answered.

"Is Larry there?" I asked.

"No, he's not here right now. Do you want to leave a message for him?"

"Yes," I hastily replied. "Tell him Debbie called. Have him call me when he returns."

"He won't be coming back until late," Peter told me.

"That's all right," I said. "I really need to talk to him. Just have him call me as soon as he gets in."

Peter promised to relay the message to Larry, and we hung up. I climbed into bed knowing that Larry would awaken me when he called me back, but it didn't matter. I had to determine if he was okay and resolve whatever was wrong. Since I had declined Larry's invitation to the banquet, there was tension and friction between us, which was understandable. I knew I'd hurt him deeply, and I felt bad. I had to make things right with him. When the phone finally rang, I was in a deep slumber and shook myself awake in order to collect my thoughts. My brain was fuzzy. I could hardly think straight, but I prayed before starting to speak.

"Are you okay?" I asked Larry. "I noticed that you weren't talking much this evening. I hope you weren't uncomfortable."

"No," Larry said. "I wasn't as uncomfortable as I was anxious to get going. Someone promised to call me this evening, and I was concerned that I'd miss the phone call."

I felt relieved when he told me that.

"I'm sorry," I said, thankful to hear his voice again. "I forgot to ask whether you were busy this evening."

"That's okay," Larry replied, and I could feel his demeanor soften slightly. There was a skip to his spirit.

I plodded on. "I haven't seen you in statistics class recently. I know that you really wanted to take me to the banquet. I'm sorry I didn't go with you, but I needed time to pray about things." I paused before continuing. "I don't want our friendship to end. I still want to talk to you."

I could audibly hear the sigh of relief as he released the breath he'd been holding.

"I appreciate your call!" he said. I could envision an enormous smile spreading across his face. Enthusiasm and joy returned to his voice. The tension that had built up between us melted away. I was glad I'd spoken to Larry and could visualize the sparkle in his eyes when he realized all was not lost with me. It was then that he resolved even harder to win me over. It was a wonderful conclusion to our final days of that school year. Spring quarter was drawing to a close. Soon, we'd all be traveling home for summer vacation. What a pleasant thought that was. Finally, I'd receive the quality sleep I needed. After I finished my final exam, I was sprinting to the dorm when I suddenly heard someone shouting my name from across campus. I turned to see Larry waving at me.

"I'm taking my final exam," he bellowed with a huge grin on his face.

"Good luck!" I shouted. "Have a wonderful summer!"

19

A NEW SCHOOL YEAR

After arriving home, I rested and relaxed for several days before beginning my summer job as a gardener at a hospital. I loved working in the hospital's perennial garden. It was such peaceful, relaxing work, and it was a blessing to be outside again after being confined indoors during most of the school year. My responsibility that steamy summer was to maintain the flowerbeds. As the summer progressed, I was also presented with the opportunity to perfect my pruning skills. My supervisor arranged for me to prune practically every tree and shrub on the premise. I pruned over sixty crab apple trees, arborvitae hedges, junipers, snowball bushes, and coniferous hedges. Ladders became a constant in my life, and dangly caterpillars brought sharp, shrill screams on an almost daily basis. Despite the crawling creatures and the frightening, beady-eyed crayfish that joined me one day, I survived.

Work kept me busy, and by the time I returned home at the end of a day, I was exhausted. My energy lagged that summer. The stress and pressure of my final quarter had worn me out. My body craved sleep. At night, I dreamed about Larry (but thankfully never about whiskery creatures with reddish-brown exoskeletons). As the summer slipped by, I found myself counting down the days until classes started again. I hadn't written many letters to my friends during the vacation and was impatient and eager to talk with them again. I was also curious to see how the roommate situation would work out.

At the end of spring quarter, my friends and I decided which dormitory rooms to reserve for the following school year. Since Isabel and I were juniors, we had a high enough class standing to obtain rooms on the newer wing of the women's dormitory. Of course, Emilia also ached for a room on the newer wing, but because she only had sophomore status, her probability of getting a room on that side was slim. Emilia developed a strategy. She figured that if Isabel and I reserved a suite, then she or Sophie would be one of our roommates. Since neither Sophie nor Emilia had the upper-class status to reserve a room on the newer wing, this provided them both with the opportunity for a room on the nicer side of Lamson Hall.

"Would you be my roommate?" Emilia asked me one day during our roommate discussions. Thankfully, Maria was in the room when she inquired.

"That wouldn't work!" Maria piped up before I could even respond. "You two are too different. You'd get on each other's nerves."

I knew that was true. Being in such close proximity to Emilia would be difficult. I needed peace and quiet and lots of alone time. Emilia didn't. We were excellent friends. I just hoped that nothing would interfere with that.

"Are you sure the roommate situation will work out?" Maria asked. She was just as concerned as I was.

"I think the two quieter people, Sophie and Debbie, should room together," Isabel wisely said one day. In the end, Sophie and I signed up to be roommates. We figured that, if we needed to, we could trade roommates later.

I wondered how the roommate situation would work out. Although I was hesitant about it, I didn't know anyone else to room with. Maria planned on becoming a student missionary, so I couldn't room with her. Another one of my friends, Lauren, was in Spain. Although I had considered the possibility of rooming with her, I didn't have time to write and ask her.

Several things had changed by the time I arrived at school that fall. For one thing, I discovered from Emilia that Isabel would be living off campus. That meant that someone was without a roommate. Secondly, I discovered that Sophie was planning on rooming with Emilia instead of me. I was surprised when Emilia informed me of that plan, but I didn't think much more about it. My mom traveled with me when I returned to Andrews that autumn so she could help with unloading. I loved my new room. For the first time, I had a campus view rather than a courtyard view. It was much nicer. The room was larger as well. As I organized my belongings, I chatted with Emilia. It really was good to see her again. Gradually, my room began taking shape.

Larry phoned shortly after my arrival. I was surprised he called. Evidently, he'd spoken to his informant, Emilia, who promptly notified him of my return.

"What are you doing?" he asked almost immediately, picking up right where we left off at the end of the preceding school year.

"Oh, I'm organizing my belongings and moving myself in," I said.

As usual, he was looking for entertainment as well as an opportunity to help me with something.

"Who is it?" Emilia asked when she overheard me talking to someone on the phone.

"It's Larry," I replied.

"Can I talk to him?" she asked as she entered my room.

I handed her the phone.

"What are you doing?" I heard her saying. "Would you like to come over and help me bunk my beds?"

Larry agreed to help, which I was grateful for since we needed help bunking the beds. My mom and I realized that after the fiasco we'd had attempting to bunk my beds earlier that day. When my mom and I would get together to do anything serious like that, we inevitably ended up in stitches of laughter, which is in no way helpful. How could anyone bunk a bed when they are laughing so uncontrollably that they can hardly stand, let alone attempt to lift a bed? When Emilia heard our deafening shrieks, she realized that my mom and I were not a fit pair to bunk her beds. We were like Abbott and Costello. I'm sure our crazy antics would have inspired laughter from anyone who happened to be walking by.

I was in my room working when Larry arrived. I could hear him talking with Emilia. For some reason, the wall that separated the two rooms amplified everything. It was almost like a microphone was hidden in the wall that separated the two rooms.

"Hello," I heard Larry say when he popped his head into my room. I invited him in but gestured for him to be quiet since my mom was sleeping.

Larry walked over to my window to soak in my magnificent view of the baseball field. Although a nearby tree restricted the view, it really wasn't unpleasant. Brilliant afternoon sunshine streamed through my window, brightening my room.

"I wish our windows opened," I told Larry. "They're still putting in new windows that open. It seems like they've been working on it for a long time. They started that project during my freshman year."

"I can fix that by throwing a rock hard enough to break the window," Larry teased. "Then they'd have to fix it."

"Yeah," I said, laughing. "They'd have no choice."

Eventually, Emilia joined us. But when we started getting noisy, I heard my mom stirring; I'd forgotten she was sleeping.

"Let's head over to your room, Emilia, so we don't wake up my mom. She isn't feeling very good, and she really needs her rest. She's exhausted!"

After we settled into Emilia's room, I informed them about my mom. "She managed a business. The pressures of her work were stressful, and she was often discouraged. This summer, she often came home in tears. My brother and I encouraged her to quit. She was worried about leaving, since we both have college expenses, but she finally did. Now she really needs rest."

After patiently listening, Larry said, "I'm glad your mom made the decision to quit her job."

"It may mean I can't attend Andrews next quarter," I said. "I'm thankful, though, that my mom can recuperate. She couldn't keep going the way she's been working. God will lead. I just have to keep trusting in Him."

Emilia and Larry shared about their summer adventures, but I could see that Larry was becoming increasingly nervous about being in our dorm room. He was afraid he'd get in trouble for being in the girls' dormitory.

"Relax," Emilia told him, attempting to calm him down. "There's hardly anyone here. Nobody will really think about it since so many people are moving in. If anyone asks any questions, we'll just tell them that you're helping us. Besides, the deans already approved for you to come up and help."

Just then, someone knocked on Emilia's door. Larry jumped. He darted into the bathroom, attempting to hide.

Emilia opened the door. "Hi," we heard her saying as I peered around the corner of the bathroom and saw one of our Hispanic housekeepers.

"It's just the housekeeper," I whispered to Larry, endeavoring to calm his fears. A few minutes later, she left, and we heard her noisy vacuum zooming down the hallway.

Noticing Larry's anxiety, I said, "Let's get the beds bunked so Larry can leave."

With Larry's assistance, bunking the beds was completed with ease.

"My mom and I tried to help, but we couldn't stop laughing," I told Larry.

"Yeah," Emilia jumped in. "I couldn't believe it. I had to go over and help them. They wouldn't have ever bunked the beds if I hadn't come along."

She was right. We would have been at a loss without Emilia's and Larry's help. I was thankful to have good friends who always came to my rescue when I needed them.

20

THE DUNES

Berrien was a place of tremendous beauty with many lakes and beaches. One of the main attractions was the Warren Dunes, a beach with lusty, colossal mounds of sand. The abundant heaps of sand arose like mountains. One Sabbath afternoon, a few of us traveled to the dunes after church. As we clambered up the scalding sand, we chatted. The dunes were the most spectacular place for adventure. I truly enjoyed spending time there.

It was a radiant day with cloudless azure skies. Standing at the summit of the enormous sand mound was amazing. The view was breathtaking. The skies were always so clear in Michigan. Beauty surrounded us. As we sprinted downward and plummeted from the mountain, it felt like we were soaring birds.

"I feel like I'm flying!" I said to Larry

"I do, too!" he replied. "I always do when I go down."

As we tumbled down the hill, Emilia's niece complained that her ankle was hurting. We helped guide her to my car that was in the parking lot at the foot of the dunes. Larry, who was genuinely concerned, attentively examined her ankle. It was swollen, and I noticed an intense look of concern spread across his face.

"You need ice. It's swollen. You should soak it in the cold water from the lake. Here, I'll carry you there," he said as he expertly lifted her up on his shoulders.

Watching, I admired the compassion and concern Larry had for Emilia's niece. It just confirmed my belief that he'd make an excellent father and an outstanding physical therapist. He always sensed when others were hurting and eagerly helped them. When we reached the beach, Larry lifted her off his broad shoulders and soaked her ankle in the chilly lake. Hopefully, she'd receive relief from her pain. Once she'd been attended to, I asked Larry if he wanted to go running along the beach. He happily agreed. We jogged for quite a while and then suddenly observed how far away we were from the others. We decided to return and slowed our pace to a trot so we could chat. It was so pleasurable talking with Larry again. I'd really missed him during the summer.

Shortly before we joined everyone, Larry plotted a strategy to throw Emilia into the lake. I agreed to help. We developed a plan that we thought would work. It probably would have, too, if I'd been stronger, taller, and heavier so I could withstand Emilia's strength. But, being petite and short, I unfortunately couldn't. While we were fiercely battling, I realized how strong Emilia really was as she flung me into the water. When I discovered myself sprawling into the lake, I was more determined than ever to get Emilia wet as well. Somehow, I managed to propel her in, but it sure wasn't easy. By the end of the intense battle, both Emilia and I were dripping wet. Larry somehow managed to stay out of it. Maybe he decided not getting wet or interfering with the fierce battle would be better. Whatever the case, I regret not throwing him in as well. After all, it was his idea.

PHILOSOPHICAL THOUGHTS

I was ecstatic to be back at Andrews that quarter. Emilia and I were managing to get along; perhaps it was because I had an intense desire to practice my Spanish. Whatever the case, we were doing more together than I ever could have imagined. When I needed to study, I'd tell Emilia. If she didn't take the hint, I'd shove her forcefully out of my room and lock the door. Usually, that was effective.

"Guess what Larry said tonight," Emilia told me smiling broadly as she dashed into my room one evening. "He said, 'I have decided that there are two types of people in the world: those who flirt and those who don't. Sophie's definitely the type who flirts. I've seen her doing it. Debbie, on the other hand, is the type who doesn't. Emilia, you don't really flirt, but you come from a cultural background that makes you more affectionate towards your friends. You often touch or hug them. Other people who are unfamiliar with your culture might think that you were flirting. Isabel, well, she's more difficult to classify. Isabel fits into both categories. She's in a category all her own.'"

I smiled as Emilia told me what Larry said. Evidently, Larry had been in an extremely philosophical mood. That was Larry all right. He brought continual laughter to me. Maybe it was a crazy thought, but it was true that generally individuals do belong to one category or the other. As Emilia droned on, a deeper feeling for Larry stirred within me. I admired the fact that he shared his thoughts so transparently with others. Although I pondered things like that sometimes, generally they never got further than pen and paper. I appreciated the fact that Larry was so open about everything.

During that quarter, Emilia teased me on multiple occasions about Larry. I think she was impatient and eager to see us get together, and she was always attempting to brew up some way to facilitate it. When Emilia's classmates and friends started questioning her about whether she and Larry were dating because they spent so much time together, she began avoiding him in an attempt to thwart gossip.

"That's ridiculous," I told her when I found out. "People always talk, but that's no reason to be so mean to Larry. Avoiding him isn't going to help. Besides," I said, "he really needs our friendship."

Emilia then began dropping sly hints about me dating Larry. Although the thought didn't bother me, I didn't convey that message to her. I still perceived that Larry was struggling to accept himself. Something kept encouraging me to wait. Was it God or just a sense I had? I believed that Larry needed the support of friends more than anything else.

Larry, too, was more frequently considering the wonderful prospect of dating me. This especially became apparent one night when I was baking in my room.

"You know what Larry said to me?" Emilia asked looking over at me when she found me in my room. "He said that he couldn't see you ever getting married."

I just smiled.

When my roommate heard that, she laughed. "I don't think that's true. Just look. Debbie is baking tonight. That's proof enough."

I perceived that Larry was growing more impatient with me. As much as I admired Larry, I was also aware that something was bothering him. I sensed that a relationship would hamper his growth and ability to heal. Whatever was hurting inside, I hoped would mend as we prayed for him, encouraged him, and reached out to him. Thankfully, Larry didn't push me. He patiently waited. But truly I was the one person he yearned for.

~22~

CLASS ASSIGNMENTS

One evening, I was studying at my desk when I heard a noisy rapping on my door. I opened it and discovered the face of Julia, a tall girl with long wavy dark brown hair and beautiful black eyes who had resided in my hall the previous school year. Although I knew her name, I wasn't well acquainted with her.

"I'm going to be your roommate," she said when I opened the door.

We talked for a few minutes, and then she left to gather her belongings.

"My roommate just arrived," I yelled to Emilia and Sophie.

When Julia returned, Emilia, Sophie, and I congregated in my room asking questions. Julia shared that she was a secondary education major. She was very easy to talk to and had a calm, sweet disposition.

All of us were finally settling into a routine. Sophie, Emilia, Julia, and I were growing accustomed to our rooming situation. However, we were struggling to find quiet times when we could study. None of us had grasped how much more common distractions would be in a suite with people constantly coming in and out to chat with one another. On the other hand, having talkative friends was often helpful with my assignments for speech pathology classes. One of my assignments that quarter was to record a speech sample from someone and count the number of dysfluencies (repetitions, prolongations, and fillers such as "um") present in their speech. The assignment was given to us for the purpose of demonstrating that everyone has normal dysfluencies in their speech.

Earlier that afternoon, I borrowed a tape recorder from Emilia so I could complete the assignment. Emilia refused to let me record her, as she found my assignments to be annoying and ridiculous. Finding it impossible to acquire a willing subject, I decided it would be best to just record a conversation with one of my suitemates and delete the recording as soon as I was done with my assignment. When Julia came in the room and started chatting, I discretely pressed the record button on the tape recorder. My assignment required about fifteen minutes of conversation, so I attempted to keep the conversation going. I could tell that Julia was surprised by how much I was talking.

The next afternoon, Julia happened to walk into the room and overheard our conversation playing on the tape recorder as I was working on my assignment. "Oh, my goodness. Did you record our conversation? I can't believe you did that! You didn't even ask. What are you doing with it?"

"I'm working on an assignment for one of my classes," I said sheepishly. "I couldn't tell you that I was recording your speech, because it would have messed up the results. You might have become too nervous and probably would have become more dysfluent or you might have slowed down your speaking rate."

"I always stutter more when I speak English to Americans than I do when speaking it with my friends. I can't believe you did that. I didn't think you'd be the type of person to do that."

I felt guilty about upsetting her and assured her that I would erase the tape when I was done. I also attempted to reassure her by explaining that everyone has dysfluencies in their speech. It is totally normal. She seemed to calm down after that.

I think Julia felt unsure about me that quarter though. If I wasn't analyzing people's speech, I was doing other crazy things for my classes like going around wearing earplugs or hearing aids. The earplug experience proved to be bothersome. It was frustrating to have something crammed into my ears. The low drone of conversation was annoying, because I missed out on the majority of what was being said. I felt like an old lady. I kept asking my friends to repeat what they said or to speak up. I must have created entertainment for my friends, especially when I said things that were totally irrelevant to the topic of conversation.

The hearing aid project was especially memorable. I learned to quickly turn the volume wheel down so that sounds would enter my ear at a more tolerable loudness level. That was a switch I became an expert at reaching for as the day wore on. Besides turning down the volume when sounds were too loud, I was also accustoming myself to the fact that even the softest sounds were being amplified. It was a strange feeling.

I still remember the day I wore a hearing aid to computer science class. Emilia was sitting on the left side of me, the side that had the earplug, and I was having a difficult time understanding her even though I was wearing a hearing aid in my right ear. The fact that every few minutes someone walked into the room and the door slammed didn't help matters. Hearing aids amplify every single noise, even the rustling of papers. Understandably, Emilia was becoming increasingly more annoyed with me. She told me that she needed to trade seats with me so that I could hear her better, but instead she began shouting in the ear with the hearing aid, which made me mad. She already spoke loud enough without having to increase the intensity of her voice. On the way out of the room when the class period ended, Emilia again turned and yelled into the hearing aid. Larry, who was waiting for us, saw the angry expression on my face.

"What's going on?" he asked.

I showed him the hearing aid that I was wearing. He had witnessed the scene, and he turned to Emilia and demanded in a stern voice, "Don't do that. You'll probably cause Debbie to have hearing loss if you keep that up." Words couldn't express how appreciative I was to Larry for coming to my defense.

Even though the speech pathology assignments didn't always go smoothly, I was grateful for my friends' support. Each assignment was helpful in teaching me the skills I use every day in my profession. Learning what it was like to have impaired hearing and learning to use assistive devices was also an essential part of my training as a therapist. I don't know where I would be today without the help of my friends.

~23~

EXTREME EXHAUSTION

The quarter was progressing fairly well, except for one thing: my energy level was significantly lagging. I knew something was wrong, but I continued pressing myself to complete homework and study for tests. Once in a while, I mentioned to Emilia and Sophie that I was tired. Typically, I ignored it but one weekend, I slept around the clock, and my friends expressed concern and wondered if I was sick.

Even Larry verbalized his concern one afternoon when he called. He knew I wasn't myself. "Why don't you go see a doctor?" he suggested.

"I think it's just a result of staying up too late. But if I don't feel better by the end of the week, I'll go see a doctor," I promised.

"I think it's more than just staying up late," Larry said. "Every time I call, you are either sleeping or tired. Something is wrong. I'm glad you're considering going to see a doctor." His persuasive tone told me he was deeply concerned.

One Friday afternoon three weeks into the quarter, the periodic weariness and exhaustion I'd been feeling washed over me with even more intensity. I just ached to collapse into bed. If it hadn't been for the field trip my professor scheduled to learn about assistive listening technology for the hearing impaired, I probably would have. Although I was interested in the topic, that day my extreme fatigue blotted out all possible interest in assistive listening devices. The vast assortment of equipment and explanations gave me an intense headache. All I yearned for was my bed. I couldn't wait to leave. After we finished the tour, all of us piled into cars. While my classmates discussed their classes and graduate school, I dozed in and out of sleep, only occasionally catching pieces of their conversation. Finally, we arrived at Lamson Hall.

Julia was talking on the phone when I returned that afternoon. I sat down my books and glanced at a note Emilia had left. Apparently, Larry called.

I walked next door to talk to my suitemates. "Emilia, what did Larry want?" I asked.

"I'm not exactly sure," she said. "He's been trying to reach you all afternoon. Why don't you call him back?"

Emilia and I chatted for a while and then she asked what my plans were for the evening.

"My only plan is to go to bed. I just want to sleep." I was too exhausted to think about accomplishing anything else. I decided to call Larry back before heading to bed.

"Where have you been?" he asked with concern.

"I had a field trip for one of my classes this afternoon," I said.

"Do you want to go for a walk?" he asked.

"I'd love to go for a walk, but right now I simply can't. I'm too exhausted. I've got to sleep."

"What are you doing this evening?"

"I don't really have any plans," I said. "All I want to do tonight is sleep."

"What are you planning to do on Sabbath?"

"I'm sleeping," I said again with a feeling of remorse knowing Larry was lonesome.

"Boy, you sure sound boring," he teased.

I laughed. It probably did sound boring. I felt terrible because I knew he was eager to do something with me, but I was also aware that I'd make a very poor companion that evening. I slumbered around the clock again that weekend. I was too exhausted to go to church, so I stayed in bed and slept. Emilia appeared a few times to chat with me or tease me. "Are you still sleeping?" she'd ask.

Later that afternoon, I visited with my friend Lauren, who I'd known since my freshman year and become better acquainted with when we spent a year together in Spain. I was eager to talk with someone and to escape the confines of my room. Thankfully, Lauren answered the door when I knocked.

"Would you like to take a walk?" she asked peering out of the window of her dorm room. "It's such a beautiful autumn day."

"Sure," I said, finally feeling ready to go outside.

Lauren was concerned when I told her about my extreme tiredness.

"Maybe a walk will help," she said smiling.

"I sure hope so," I replied

The autumn air felt crisp and cool, and the skies were clear and luminous. The trees blazed with brilliant hues of red, orange, and yellow. The radiant sun was streaming from the sky and everything around us was beautiful. It was wonderful to communicate with Lauren again. I'd really missed her the year before when she was living in Spain. After our stroll, we collected some of the gorgeous autumn leaves as a keepsake. We had an amusing time scuffing through the massive mounds of falling leaves. The entire experience invigorated us. The air was growing chillier, and the gleaming sun was beginning its descent as we walked back to the dorm. I was feeling more refreshed.

That weekend, I started to feel the pressure and stress of the upcoming busy week of tests but I felt my stamina lagging and found it difficult to study. I kept falling asleep. As the first day of tests ended, I breathed a sigh of relief. I was studying for the remaining two tests when I became drowsy. As was normally my custom, I decided to go jogging. Usually, that provided me with more energy, but when I returned I felt even more exhausted. It was all I could do to thrust one foot ahead of the other and ascend the flight of steps leading to my room.

Emilia appeared in my room shortly after I arrived. As usual, she just ached to talk. When she saw me, she immediately noticed my extreme exhaustion. "Some exercise might help," she said.

"I just went jogging and I feel worse," I replied.

A concerned look crossed her face and she asked, "Have you seen a doctor?"

With her and Larry's insistence, I decided I would go to the doctor later in the week. I was beginning to believe that their concern was valid and that I really was sick.

That evening, I found it difficult to study. I just ached to go to bed. Even the thought of failing my tests didn't bother me. For the first time in my life, I just felt like giving up. Sophie encouraged me. "You would probably be better off taking the tests tomorrow. At least you'd get the tests over with so they wouldn't be hanging over your head. You've already studied for them, so you won't fail."

I was thankful for her wisdom and encouragement. Without these friendships, I'm not sure I would have made it through that difficult period. They kept me sane and gave me the courage and strength I needed to persevere.

MONO

Exhaustion was the word that best described the way I felt that quarter. I simply couldn't shake it. One morning, I tried to get up to go to class, but a few minutes later I crawled back on my bed to rest. Just standing completely wore me out. I knew something was wrong, but what? Finally, I phoned my mom. I just needed to talk. Immediately, my mom knew that something was wrong.

"I just want to give up on everything," I told her. "I'm so tired. I don't have energy to study. All I want to do is sleep."

My mom listened and attempted to encourage me. She told me that she would phone my aunt who lived only a few minutes away from the university and would call me right back. When she called the second time, she said, "Don't go anywhere. Just stay in bed and rest. She will come over as soon as she can. Did you get the results back from the doctor?"

"No," I said. "They're supposed to be back today."

"Well, I'll call the doctor and see if they've received the results," she said.

Eventually, my aunt arrived and brought a package and encouraged me. "Don't give up," she insisted. "Your teachers will work with you," she reassured me. I appreciated her visit and encouragement.

Finally, the results of my labs came in. I tested positive for mono, and within a few short hours immediate changes were made. I met with the dean, and she assisted me with finding a room where I could get more rest. My mom decided that she would travel up that weekend to help me move. On Sunday when my mom arrived, I was so thankful to see her and grateful for her help.

A few minutes after my mom arrived, Larry phoned and offered to help, which I gladly accepted. With everyone's assistance, I quickly settled into my new, homier room. Even now, all these years later, I still remember that room. It was extremely tiny. When my mom and I first entered it, we wondered how we'd ever fit all my belongings inside. Every wall contained furniture: a bed, a small six-foot-wide closet, a dresser, a wall heater, a desk, and a bookshelf. There was one large window in the room that my twin bed was positioned under. My bed and closet took up an entire wall. We couldn't fit all my things inside. The room was simply too tiny, so my mom traveled home with all of my unessential items. As the days slowly slipped by, I became more accustomed to my new dorm room. The peace and quiet proved to be exactly what I needed. With rest, I could finally tackle my studies with more motivation. It seemed strange, though, not to see Emilia and Sophie. I missed living with my friends, but I was too exhausted to think much about it.

One day shortly after my move, Emilia handed me a note from Larry. On the outside, Larry had drawn a picture of himself and a word bubble that said, "Get well, or else. (Or else you'll really be sick.)" As I unfolded the note, I discovered a disk that he'd borrowed. Inside it read, "So I'm too cheap to get a card. Hope you're okay."

As the quarter progressed, Larry began calling more and more frequently to see how things were going. Whenever he phoned, we'd always end up chatting for an incredibly long time. I always looked forward to his calls. They boosted my spirits. During one conversation, I told Larry, "I'm planning on turning off the ringer on my phone when I sleep so nobody will disturb me." I knew if I didn't that someone would wake me up and interrupt my sleep.

"That's a good idea," he said. "It's better than getting angry at the person who wakes you up." Always incredibly thoughtful, Larry began calling earlier in the evening so he wouldn't disturb my sleep.

As the quarter progressed, I began caring less and less about my appearance. I was too exhausted to worry. It was hard enough to wake up in the morning. The thought of wearing nice clothes and fixing my hair wasn't very pleasant. I dressed up only when absolutely necessary, which wasn't very often. When I think about it now, it makes me laugh. It turns out that I wasn't alone. As I discovered later from Emilia, Sophie had also contracted mono shortly after I did, and she was doing the same thing.

"Sophie sleeps in the same pair of jogging pants that she wears to class," Emilia said. "She just hops out of bed, shakes the wrinkles out of her clothes, grabs her books, and heads to class."

When Sophie and I heard comments like this, we'd just look at each other and start laughing. We knew it seemed silly, but when you feel as rotten as we did you learn what to do to survive. Both Julia and Emilia were appalled by Sophie's "lack of hygiene" as they termed it. But neither of them could truly understand just how extremely horrible a person with mono can feel. If they had experienced the illness, maybe they would have been more understanding and sympathetic. We were simply doing the best we could to push through our illness and finish our college classes.

Thankfully, Larry was very understanding, and his phone calls helped make the difficulties I was facing with my illness more tolerable. He was the bright spot of that quarter. Talking to Larry gave my days meaning. I just couldn't imagine what my life would have been like without him. And I didn't even want to try to think about that.

~25~

A COMPLIMENT

One Sunday, Larry phoned and asked what I was doing.

"I'm in the midst of chaos." I had everything spread out all over my room. "I'm trying to come up with ideas for a therapy session I have to do tomorrow. My teacher is pretending to be a client. I'm scared about it. This is the first therapy session that I've ever done."

"Don't worry. You'll do fine," Larry enthusiastically replied.

"I hope so," I responded.

We chatted for a while longer and then Larry asked, "Will you be busy later? I need to go to the store."

"I can take you," I replied, and we settled on a time.

The day of my first therapy session finally arrived. Feeling better, I carefully dressed up in professional attire and meticulously groomed my hair. As the minutes ticked by, my nervousness intensified as my therapy session drew nearer. I hoped I'd have enough materials. Several of my classmates uttered the same fears when I arrived at class, so I knew I wasn't alone. Finally, my name was called. It was time for me to begin. Amazingly, it went much more smoothly than I'd anticipated. I actually had fun. I breathed a sigh of relief when it was over.

After class, I strolled over to my computer science class. Spotting Larry, I sat down beside him. As soon as he noticed me, he responded with eyes sparkling, "You really look nice."

"Thanks!" I replied.

"What did you do to your hair today?" he asked. "It really looks good."

I laughed. "I actually fixed it today. The last few weeks I haven't bothered to do anything with it. I just haven't had much energy to dress up."

Following that conversation, I resolved to spend more time getting ready in the morning. If Larry made such a big deal about my appearance, it was evident that I hadn't been looking too great during the last few weeks. Even Emilia had begun teasing me about my appearance. She would say, "Didn't you wear those pants yesterday?" or "Your socks don't match." I'd say in the loudest whisper possible without disrupting the class, "I don't care." Following Larry's statement, though, I figured that I'd better start dressing up more so I didn't look so scruffy all of the time.

My friends provided me with the strength and courage to succeed that quarter despite my illness. Being in that small room away from other people also provided me with the rest I needed so I could focus on my studies. Despite my lagging energy level that quarter, I was being exposed to courses that I loved. One of my favorites was my fluency class. I was learning all about the different types of dysfluencies and how to treat fluency disorders. I also had to go somewhere and stutter to someone so I could understand what it felt like emotionally to have this speaking issue. Despite my illness and difficulties, God was helping me make it through that quarter successfully so I could learn the skills I needed to become the professional that I am today.

During that quarter, Sophie often came to my room to talk. I think the fact that we were going through the same experiences with our illness drew us together. We continued to encourage each other and often prayed together, asking for God's strength to help us make it through the quarter. Sophie especially needed God's strength as she had a more severe case of mono than I did and she'd missed two weeks of classes trying to recover. She dropped one course and received an incomplete grade in another so she could catch up on her assignments. Fortunately, God was seeing her through it all.

At the beginning of the quarter, Sophie's aunt said, "Sophie, I think you will start dating someone this year." Her prediction came to fruition. Sophie became acquainted with Rob in the cafeteria at the beginning of that quarter. Rob had noticed that Sophie was missing for two weeks when she went to live at her aunt's house while she recovered from her illness. When Sophie returned to school following those two weeks, Rob invited Sophie out for a date. That became the highlight of the quarter for Sophie! Soon, she and Rob were dating. His presence helped Sophie deal with the symptoms of her illness and the pressures of catching up on her classes. Thanks to Rob, Sophie survived that rough quarter. Indeed, God was providing for her needs.

~26~

LAUREN

As the quarter progressed, I began spending more time with Lauren. My new room was closer to hers, so it was easier to visit with each other. Often, she would come down to visit, and we'd share verses from the Bible that we'd come across in our devotions. They were a great source of encouragement to us. In the afternoons, I would often hear a noisy knock on my door and discover Lauren standing there when I opened the door. She'd inform me about her tests or discuss all the things that happened to her during the day. One day, she told me a comical story about something that had happened to her that morning. She had been planning to go to the academy to observe and assist a teacher as a way of fulfilling one of her requirements for an introduction to teaching class. Exhausted, she couldn't wake up that morning, so she stayed in bed until the last minute and hurriedly bustled around to get ready.

"I ran all the way to the academy," she told me. "When I got there, nobody was there. Then I remembered there was no school that day for the academy students. I just started laughing. I could just see God laughing with me. By the time I returned to my room, I was refreshed and ready to study."

I still kept in touch with Emilia, too, but being in a different room didn't provide me with as many opportunities to see her. I knew she missed my visits, but our schedules were so different that it made it challenging to visit with her. Early one morning, I was rushing to class when I felt someone grab me around the neck and give me a hug. I was attacked with such force that I nearly fell to the ground. Turning around, I saw Emilia grinning at me. I could tell that she was pleased to see me.

"I know that you're glad to see me, but do you have to throw me on the ground?" I teased.

I found that the best way for me and Emilia to keep in touch was by phone, and every once in a while when I needed a break, I would call her. One evening when I phoned her, I was in a crazy mood. I had been studying intensely, which sometimes made me so delirious that I would start laughing uncontrollably.

"How are you doing?" I asked and began laughing uncontrollably. "I just thought I'd brighten your day. I'm tired of studying and need a break."

Obviously, Emilia wasn't in a pleasant mood, or at least she didn't wish to be bothered by the likes of me. "Why don't you call Larry and talk to him," she said. A second later, the phone went dead. Emilia must have called Larry, because a few minutes later the phone rang, and Larry was on the other end. By the time he called, I had stopped laughing and had calmed down and we had a nice conversation.

I enjoyed talking to Larry. It provided a much-needed break, and my sanity was once again returning. Whenever I was worried about a test, he'd always tell me, "I'm sure you'll do fine." He was usually right. I just needed to hear those words from him. He was always the calm in the middle of my storms in life.

27

MICROBIOLOGY CULTURES

One afternoon, Larry phoned. He was tremendously discouraged. Evidently, his microbiology lab hadn't gone very well that day, and he was extremely upset about it.

"Nothing worked out right!" he confided. "I was a klutz. I think I broke an entire box of lab slides today. I kept having to redo everything. My lab partner, Kevin, and I did cultures from our arms and mouth to determine whether the soap, toothpaste, and mouthwash we use are effective in removing microorganisms. Guess what happened? On everyone else's samples, nothing showed up, but what do you suppose happened to my samples?" he inquired with signs of frustration in his voice. "Mine contained a huge assortment of bacteria. I don't understand. Why am I the only person who has so many types of bacteria on my cultures? Maybe I should start scouring myself. It's disgusting to think that I produce so much bacteria. I think I'd better switch the soap and toothpaste that I'm using, too."

"What toothpastes are most effective in reducing bacteria?" I asked.

"Colgate works the best," Larry said. "Why, what toothpaste do you use?"

"I either use Aquafresh or Crest," I said.

"I can't remember whether Aquafresh kills bacteria," he replied. "I think Crest does. After my experiment, though, I'm hesitant to believe that Aquafresh works. I do know that Colgate works the best. I highly suggest that you use it."

As we talked, Larry calmed down. Our conversation continued for quite a while that evening. Larry was extremely talkative, and I, too, was chatting almost as much. Many times in our conversations, Larry would tell me that he wished it would snow. "I love the snow," he'd say. "The more snow there is, the better it is."

"Well," I teased, "just don't do a snow dance. I like the beauty of the snow, too, but I'm not nearly as anxious as you are for snowy weather to arrive. Winter will bring enough snow as it is."

I heard silence on the other end, and visions of our sledding escapades entered my mind. Maybe winter weather wouldn't be so bad.

28

A SPECIAL BIRTHDAY

L ate one brisk autumn evening, Larry called.

"What are you doing?" he asked. "Am I interrupting your sleep?" His voice showed signs of deep concern.

"No, I haven't made it to bed yet," I replied, pleased to talk to him.

A sigh of relief came through the receiver of the phone. "Would you be willing to take me to the store?" he asked.

"Sure, but not tonight," I said. "I've already gotten ready for bed."

"Well, I'll tell you what. Tomorrow is your birthday, right? If you take me to the store tomorrow, I'll take you out to eat for your birthday. Does that sound like a fair deal?" he asked.

"Yes," I quickly replied. "That's fine. I'll take you tomorrow."

"Where do you want to go eat?" He wanted me to choose.

"Let me think about it. I don't have any ideas right now."

My residence adviser suddenly opened my door to sign me in for the evening. She was surprised to discover that I was still awake. Larry and I continued chatting after she left. It was exceptionally late when we finally hung up. Despite my late night, I managed to wake up early the next day. The fact that it was my birthday and the prospect of going out to eat with Larry provided me with the extra energy I needed to wake up. I was eager to discover what was in the birthday packages my parents had mailed me.

Leaping out of bed, I grabbed the presents that were hidden under my bed. I had barely started unwrapping the first one when my phone rang. I realized it was probably my mom, so I hurriedly scrambled for the phone.

"Happy Birthday!" my mom exclaimed. "Have you opened your presents?"

"No," I replied. "I was just starting to before you called."

"Well, open them!" she commanded. "I want to tell you about them."

There were three packages, and they all felt squishy. "I bet it's clothes," I said out loud thinking about my mom's good taste. "What else could it be?"

"Well, you'll just have to see."

Inside each box, I discovered beautiful clothing: a gorgeous soft white cotton blouse, a dark turquoise turtleneck, and a cotton floral skirt.

"Thank you!" I said. "I really like the outfit. I love everything from Laura Ashley!" My mom knew that I particularly loved that store, but the expensive prices didn't permit me to purchase clothes there very frequently.

"I knew that you needed a new winter church dress," my mom said. "I hope you like the color. I wasn't sure if you would, so I left the tags on so you can exchange them if you want."

"I love the colors! It will be wonderful to have something new to wear. Thank you," I said, then hurried off to my morning classes.

In computer science that morning, I cheerfully waved to Larry. He asked me to meet him after assembly that afternoon. After class, I raced over to the financial aid office to see if the financial aid forms I'd submitted earlier that quarter were finally processed. I also wanted to find out if they'd determined my eligibility status. When I arrived, I was surprised to discover that Lauren's cheerful, outgoing dad was there as well. When he noticed me, he immediately started a conversation with me. Lauren had mentioned that he was traveling down that weekend, but I'd forgotten. We talked while we waited. Finally, I heard my name being called, announcing that it was my turn. When I asked how much financial aid I was eligible for during winter quarter, they showed me the numbers. I almost started crying. There would be no way for me to remain at Andrews the following quarter. My mom was still unemployed, so she couldn't assist me financially. I was brokenhearted.

Lauren's dad, who was a pastor, followed me out of the office, endeavoring to provide some encouragement. "Sometimes things seem so discouraging," he said. "But remember everything is in God's hands. I don't know why He's allowing this to happen, but you must trust that He knows what's best!" He prayed with me and then gave me a hug. I thanked him. I was delighted and pleased that he'd arrived when he did. I truly had needed some encouragement.

I strolled back to my room, attempting to gather myself together. I set my books down and promptly phoned Larry. Nobody answered, so I decided to call my informant Emilia to ask if she'd seen Larry.

"Where have you been?" she asked. "Larry's been looking all over for you. Have you tried looking in the lobby? He was there a few minutes ago."

By the time I entered the lobby and found Larry, I had calmed down considerably and was at least capable of smiling. I didn't feel like talking about what I'd learned that morning, since it was such a depressing thought, so I simply pushed the thought aside attempting to focus on happier things.

"Hi," Larry said when he saw me in the lobby. "Where have you been?"

"I had to go to the financial aid office. Sorry you had so much difficulty finding me," I replied resolving not to inform him about the terrible news I'd received.

"Oh yeah, I guess you told me that you'd be going there today. I forgot. I didn't even think about looking there. Don't worry about it," he said. "I should have set a location to meet last night when we were talking on the phone. It didn't cross my mind though."

As we headed to my car, I asked Larry where he'd like to go.

"I told you that I'd take you wherever you wanted to go," Larry reminded me.

"Well," I said, "the only place I could come up with was a Chinese restaurant."

"That's fine," he replied.

"Do you like Chinese food?" I inquired.

"I'm not sure. I haven't had it before, but I'm willing to try it if that's where you want to go."

So, we traveled over to the restaurant. It had been a long while since I'd eaten Chinese food, so I was looking forward to it. On our way there, I said, "Sorry about not taking you to the store last night. I was too tired and ready for bed. I hope you didn't mind."

"No," he replied. "It gave me a good excuse to take you out to eat for your birthday."

Music was playing quietly in the background when we entered the dimly lit restaurant. Only a few people were in the room eating. We were seated quickly and when the waitress came to take our order, Larry asked for some suggestions. "Is egg foo young very good?"

"Yes, if you like eggs and vegetables." I described to him what it was. When I told him that I thought he'd like it, he decided to order it. Larry was interested in trying everything. When he spied the tea on the table, he tried it. He took a sip of it first to decide whether he liked it.

"Well, it's not bad," he stated. "Do you want some?"

"No, that's okay. I don't like tea very much. I usually only drink herbal teas."

He finished the rest of the cup and poured some more tea for himself. My resolve not to inform Larry about my discovery that morning didn't last for long.

"Today when I went to the financial aid office, I learned that I won't get enough aid to attend Andrews winter quarter. I hate to think about it!" I said gloomily. "I'm really going to miss everyone."

Most of all though, I thought to myself, *I'll really miss you, Larry.* That was why I'd become so distressed and miserable earlier that morning. I didn't want to go home. I'd miss his lengthy daily phone calls. I couldn't afford the long-distance phone calls, so it would be harder to keep in touch with him. I briskly changed the conversation to a more pleasant and enjoyable subject. Larry had been enthusiastically chatting with me about getting an apartment. He was excited about the idea of living off campus.

"Have you come up with any off-campus apartments yet?" I asked.

"No, I still have to talk to my friends," he said.

We had a pleasant time together, and the meal was delicious. Larry was inquisitive about everything and seemed to savor every minute of the experience. We chatted about our quarter and about the upcoming Christmas vacation. I ached for the conversation to continue on, not wanting it to end. It was always a blessing to spend time with Larry. A lump rose in my throat at the thought of not seeing him during winter quarter. I would miss him, but I couldn't think about that then so I pulled my thoughts back to our conversation and the gratefulness that I could spend time with him for a few more days. Soon, our meal was over and we headed off to the store so Larry could purchase the items he needed.

That evening, Emilia boisterously knocked on my door. I'd agreed to go somewhere with her that evening, although she hadn't been incredibly specific about where we were going or what we'd be doing. I was on the phone when she arrived. I'd been receiving all kinds of phone calls that afternoon. When I finally hung up, we descended the stairs to West Lobby. I was surprised to discover that the majority of my friends were there. We divided up so we could cram into cars and journey over to Isabel's apartment.

Almost as soon as I arrived, another friend and I were being gustily wished "Happy Birthday!" A few minutes later, an exquisitely decorated cake was retrieved. Then Lauren and Larry handed me a present. I was surprised to find a potholder. That would definitely come in handy. I knew that it had been Larry's idea. One day in computer class he noticed a sore on my hand and asked what happened. I told him that I'd burned myself on my toaster oven, and he told me I should be more careful.

"Now I won't burn myself. Thanks!" I said.

Larry handed me a card, and I opened it. On the outside it read: "There are two things that I want in a friendship." Inside it said, "You and me. Happy Birthday."

Isabel and Emilia handed me a large sack. "Sorry," they told me as they handed me the bag, "we didn't have time to wrap it." Inside I discovered a poster. It was a picture of a child who was in bed praying before she ate. A dog and cat were sitting on the bed, earnestly begging for some of the food. It's a picture that still hangs on the wall of my home as a reminder of those wonderful college days.

"I really like it!" I said. "This definitely fits my style. Thanks!"

That was a birthday that I would long remember. We all spent a relaxing evening chatting and playing amusing games. It was wonderful to have everyone together. All of my friends had genuinely helped to create an unforgettable day.

29

GOODBYES

The hours of the quarter were ticking by, and before I knew it, the quarter was slipping to a close. I'd just returned from an exam when the phone rang. I answered it even though I really wasn't in the mood to talk to anyone. Almost as soon as I said hello, I heard Larry's familiar cheerful voice.

"Where have you been?" I heard him asking. "I tried calling you earlier this afternoon."

"I was taking an exam. I just got back. I'm soaked. It started pouring during the exam, and I didn't have an umbrella. I was anxious to get back to my room and needed to clear my mind, so I just ran across campus as fast as I could. Now, I'm sopping wet. I probably should have waited until the rain let up."

"You should have called me," Larry said. "I have a big golf umbrella that can easily fit two people under it. Then you wouldn't have had to get wet."

I appreciated his suggestion. It would have been nice, but after the test my mind was too blurred to think very rationally.

"I don't mind running in the rain," I told Larry. "It is nicer, though, when I'm prepared for it. It's also better when there is no thunder and lightning."

Larry listened to me rattle on, and then he finally expressed his reason for calling. "Would you like to watch Hamlet with us tonight? We are going over to Isabel's to watch it."

"I'd love to, but I really need to study, especially since it's exam week. Besides, I want to go to bed early tonight. Thanks for asking though." I was pleased that Larry would finally have the opportunity to watch it. He'd been aching to see it for a long time.

Later that evening, Emilia phoned. I was surprised that she'd called so soon. "I thought you'd still be watching the movie," I said.

"Well," she told me, "we ran into some bad luck. A bolt of lightning hit the house and damaged the cable lines, so we couldn't watch the movie. Besides that, Larry lost a program that he had written for computer class when he was saving it on his computer. I guess he'll have to stay up late tonight to rewrite it." *Boy, what an evening they've had*, I thought.

Before I knew it, exams were over and the quarter had come to a close. I was in my room packing when Larry phoned.

"What are you doing?" he asked.

"Oh, I'm packing," I said.

"Hey, I'll help you if you want. I'm in East Lobby."

There was plenty that I needed help with, so I eagerly accepted his invitation and ran off to get him.

"Where'd you get the idea that I know most of the girls on campus?" Larry asked as we strolled toward my room.

I laughed thinking that I probably shouldn't have said anything to Emilia. As my personal informant, she always told Larry everything I said. "Well," I replied, "it's true. Every time we walk down the sidewalk, you say hi to everyone you pass, and then you proceed to tell me their names or something about the individual. You're definitely more outgoing than I am. I don't know even half of the people you do."

Larry said, very humbly, denying the fact, "I don't know those people very well. They are just acquaintances. I simply learn their names and stick them in a file so I can retrieve them when I need them."

"You're definitely much better at remembering people's names than I am. And you know a lot more people than I do," I replied.

We entered my room. It was beginning to take on an empty and less homey appearance. "I'm going to miss this room," I said as I plopped down on the floor. "I hate to think about leaving. I'm really going to miss everyone."

Neither of us were very anxious to work, especially after a stressful week, so we just sat and talked for a few minutes. Suddenly, Larry spied a backpack shoved under my bed. I knew I should have moved it, but I hadn't.

"What's this?" Larry asked extracting the bag.

"Never mind," I almost shouted, hastily snatching it back.

Larry laughed when I hid it under some pillows. "Now you're making me curious," he said as he gave me a questioning look of curiosity and rubbed the back of his head. He was silent for a few moments as I stared back at him desperately trying to thwart his curiosity. "You don't want to find out," I finally replied as my face reddened hoping he wouldn't persist. "It would embarrass you," I said thinking about the monthly supplies that the bag contained.

That comment stopped him. He knew that if that was the case, it would probably embarrass me as well, so he decided not to pursue his curiosity. I was grateful!

He helped me move a few of my heavy items to my car. I mostly required assistance moving my bigger belongings, but I still needed some of them. Agreeing to Larry's suggestion, I resolved to wait until the following day to move the remainder of my things, so we finally elected to amble out to the lobby to chat. Shortly after sitting down, Larry turned and asked, "Do you still think that you are overweight?" It was a surprising question, but I guess I'd mentioned something to him earlier that quarter. "I saw you hug your friend in the lobby today. You really have a cute figure," he said. I thanked him. He was always ready and willing to offer compliments to people. I really appreciated his sincerity. I knew though, that beyond his words he was also conveying a much deeper message.

The following day, Lauren and I finished packing my Mercury Lynx. It was a huge job, but with Lauren's assistance the work passed quickly.

"I sure hope I don't have to move again for a while," I told Lauren. "I don't enjoy having to move so frequently. I hardly get settled, and I'm off again."

She agreed.

Larry phoned later that morning, "Do you need help?" he asked.

"No, Lauren and I have almost finished the job. Would you like to meet us in the cafeteria for lunch?"

"Sure," he said.

Lauren, Larry, and I lingered at the lunch table. None of us were anxious to interrupt the few remaining minutes for us to chat. I think all of us were feeling the tremendous anguish and gloom of my necessary departure. I was really going to miss them! Finally, the miserable goodbyes that I'd been dreading had to be uttered. Everything was finally packed. It was time for me to go. We all leisurely strolled over to my car.

"I wish I could stay and complete the rest of the school year," I said sorrowfully.

They all nodded in agreement.

I hugged Lauren goodbye and watched her leave. Then I reached over to hug Larry. All I could manage to say was "bye." Inside, I was fighting tears and the words that I ached to say caught in my throat. Larry, as usual, didn't have any difficulty expressing his thoughts. He gingerly raised me up off the ground and squeezed me tightly in his arms.

"I've always wanted to do that," he said. It felt so good to be held by him.

His enthusiastic response caused a huge smile to cross my face. His gesture spoke volumes to me and I wished the moment could last forever. But he eventually had to let me go. Sadly, I had to leave him and climb into my car. I waved to him as I drove slowly away. He lingered. I watched his shape grow smaller and smaller as I drove away.

Even though we were both smiling on the outside, I knew that on the inside he felt the same way I did about my departure. It was the words that he didn't verbalize and the words that I was unable to express that haunted me on my trip home. Maybe the hug communicated more than mere words ever could. It was simple, but both of us knew that there was a much deeper feeling that only the hug had conveyed. It was then that I knew that Larry really did love me, and it was then that I grasped just how much I loved him. *I really am going to miss him*, I thought to myself as tears began streaming from my eyes. *I wish I didn't have to go, Lord. I pray that you will continue to protect and guide Larry.*

30

HOME AGAIN

Before the holidays began, I enrolled in a few classes at a local community college near my home. Christmas vacation zoomed by, and soon I was beginning my first day of classes at the community college. At first, it was difficult to adjust to being away from Andrews, but gradually I became accustomed to the new routine. I intensely missed Andrews and all my friends. I especially missed Larry and his frequent interruptions. In a letter to my friends, I wrote:

> It's hard to get used to going to a public college. I've gone to private schools all my life. The community college is so much bigger than I'm used to. I pass different faces every day. I feel like a fish out of water. I really miss Andrews. People are so friendly there and the school is smaller so even though I don't know everybody's name at least I know their face. Here it's the same feeling as walking down the streets of the city. I feel like a

stranger in a crowd of people. It's definitely an entirely different atmosphere than Andrews.

As the quarter progressed, I adjusted to the environment. People may not have talked much during the initial days of class, but I became acquainted with more of my classmates and began to feel less like a loner in a crowd of people. Beyond classes, I was slowly adjusting to living at home again. It was wonderful spending more time with my family, but it came with challenges. My younger brother was becoming frustrated with me invading his study space. I hogged the desk that he was accustomed to having to himself. There simply wasn't enough space for two people, especially two siblings. It became a game, or maybe a heated battle is a more appropriate word.

When my brother wanted to use the desk, he knew the one sentence that was most effective in getting me to move: "I need to use my computer." I had no choice. His computer was in the middle of the desk, so I was forced to move. When he'd open up a book and just sit there studying, I knew he'd won. "You liar," I would say. A mischievous grin would spread across his face. Then a pen fight would ensue, and we'd launch into giving each other mustaches or marks by whatever means possible. By the end, we'd always be covered in a rainbow of colors and a variety of designs. That soon became routine. Hardly a night elapsed without an amusing pen fight.

I also adored having my orange, tiger-striped cat roaming around again. I'd almost forgotten what it was like to have a pet. I would often discover him in the window waiting to greet me when I arrived home from class. I enjoyed feeling him pounce on my feet when I climbed the stairs or just hearing him prowl around the house to discover what I was accomplishing. He was my sanity that quarter. He provided me with incentive to study, and I'd lug him into the office and close the door behind me. He'd curl up on the floor and fall asleep. Sometimes he'd climb onto the desk and sprawl out on my papers while I studied. My study buddy was always close by.

Although I'd adjusted to life at home, I couldn't forget about my friends at Andrews. Larry was at the forefront of my mind. I missed him immensely. I was also becoming more anxious and eager to register for more speech pathology classes. But could I ever return? I had to find a way. An idea suddenly dawned on me. I phoned the financial aid department to see if I could apply my unused funding from the current quarter towards the spring quarter. I learned that I could, which meant there was a real possibility I could return.

One evening in February, I received a phone call from Larry. It seemed like it had been forever since we'd last spoken to each other. I'd written to him, but it wasn't enough. I thought about him continually.

"How are you doing?" Larry asked.

"Oh, I'm good," I replied. "But I'm missing everyone." (*Especially you,* I thought to myself.) "I really want to return!"

"We miss you, too," he said. "I called to wish you a happy Valentine's Day. I wanted to send you some flowers, but I spent most of my money when I went to see a friend in Chicago."

"Oh, that's okay," I said smiling, thankful to hear his voice again. "I'm just glad that you called. It's nice to talk to you again!"

"It's nice to talk to you, too," he told me.

"Guess what? I think I've found a way to attend Andrews again."

"That's wonderful news!" he replied. "I can't wait to see you again." I could envision a huge smile spread across his face at the thought.

"I can't wait to see you," I said, thankful he'd called.

It seemed like our conversation concluded all too soon. His phone call really made my day and made it even more clear that I needed to find a way to attend Andrews again. After my conversation with Larry, I began planning my return. Slowly, things fell into place. Larry must have informed Emilia I was returning, because just a few weeks later I received an unexpected phone call from Sophie. She asked me to be her roommate. I told her I would love to. We began planning and deciding on a room location. Then we discussed what things we'd need for the dorm room. It was amazing to see how things were rapidly falling into place. I knew the Lord had made it a reality.

One more thing needed to happen to solidify my plans. I called the financial aid office to ensure that I'd received the aid they'd promised I was eligible for. As seems to be the custom when plans are created, I encountered a setback. There was a delay with processing the funding I was eligible for. I was extremely upset. Now, at the last minute, they were informing me that I didn't have the money I needed to return. My mom and I composed a letter describing the problem, and we negotiated with the financial aid department. After much effort, things were finally resolved, and I was free to return. The Lord had answered my prayers.

~31~

BEAUTY AND THE BEAST

efore I knew it, I was settled back at Andrews and was registering for another quarter. After standing in lines all day, I was exhausted. As I staggered back to my room with my heavy load of books, someone silently snuck up behind me and placed their hands over my eyes. My choices were extremely limited as to who it could be. After a few seconds of thought, I knew that it had to be Larry.

"How'd you guess?" he asked.

"Well, I knew that it was either you or Emilia," I said smiling. "After some thought, I was certain that it had to be you."

"Shucks!" Larry said.

Boy, it sure was good to see Larry again! I had missed him. I noticed that he was just as pleased to see me. He had an enormous smile on his face, and his eyes were sparkling with delight. After talking for a while, Larry informed me that he and Emilia were traveling to South Bend to purchase some things at the store.

173

"Would you like to come along?" The expression on his face told me that he was eager for me to join them.

"You don't have anything else to do." he said, looking at me with pleading eyes.

"Okay. I'll go!" I exclaimed, looking forward to spending time with both of them again. "Just give me a chance to grab something to eat. I'm starving."

We arranged to meet in West Lobby. Everyone was gathered around talking when I arrived. I wondered why I had rushed around so much. They didn't appear to be in any hurry. Paul, an exceptionally talkative friend, turned to me when I entered the lobby. It had been a long while since I'd last spoken to him.

"Wow, there's Deb the Debmeister!" he said.

I found a seat beside Larry. After Paul had made his rounds conversing with everyone in the room, he meandered over to where Larry and I were seated and started talking to us.

"Are you dating anyone?" Paul asked, directing his question to me.

"No," I said a little timidly, scared to discover what his next response might be.

He turned to Larry and asked him the same question.

"No," Larry replied.

Then Paul said, "Well, why not?"

I wasn't quite sure how to respond. I wasn't really in the mood to explain. *There are several reasons*, I thought to myself. Finally, I settled on a response.

"I'm happy the way I am," I replied, hoping that he wouldn't ask for any further explanations.

"I see," Paul said thoughtfully. "You're just waiting for the right person to come along."

Well, not quite, I thought to myself. *I wouldn't mind dating Larry. I'm just waiting for the right time. God's time.*

The afternoon passed quickly. Emilia was her usual bubbly self. She had more to talk about than I could ever dream of saying. Before leaving the dorm, she suggested that I take my car. "Three people don't fit as well in my truck," she said chuckling and smiling at the recollection. "Remember when we had Maria ride in the back? I don't think that either you or Larry want to stay in the back."

I smiled, recalling how upset Maria had gotten after a long trip in the back. It really wasn't fun to be cooped up back there.

"I'll take my car," I answered. "None of us need to experience that!"

Larry, as usual, was filled with comments about my car. "I'll sit in the back," he said. "I always have to sit sideways in your car or crouch down so my head doesn't touch the ceiling. This car definitely wasn't designed for tall people. When I get a car, I want to get one that will give me plenty of head room, like a Jeep or a Samurai."

On our way back, we stopped by Larry's apartment to drop off the items that he had purchased. It also provided me with an opportunity to see his place. Larry showed me around, apologizing about the mess. I could tell that he was enjoying the freedom and independence of having his own apartment.

"It's much better than the dorm," he said, smiling contentedly. "I have lots more space, and I can finally cook for myself."

"I'm pleased you're enjoying it," I replied.

Later that week, Larry called and invited me to see *Beauty and the Beast*. I knew that Larry had been eager to see it for a long while, and I had as well.

"Enjoy yourself!" Sophie said as I left to meet Larry. "I'm glad you're going. You need the break." I knew she was right. Once school was underway, there wouldn't be as much free time. My studies could wait. Larry met me in the main lobby of Lamson Hall, and we drove to a small town near the college. The drive was a pleasant one. The trees were alive with gorgeous, pungent spring blossoms, and the view was breathtaking. Spring was one of my favorite seasons. I loved the pastel glow of the trees and the sunlit breezy days.

As we entered the sparsely filled theatre and found our seats, I watched and thought. As always, it was wonderful being with Larry. The movie was amazing. It was a simple story, yet its message was one that I strongly believed in. We often look at the external beauty and appearances of a person and make judgments, which can sometimes impact our ability to become better acquainted with someone. We must learn instead from the Bible's image of beauty: "Man looks on the outward appearance, but the Lord looks at the heart." (I Samuel 16:7) This is something that we should all strive to do. Maybe God provided me with this insight as a young child, because this has always been something I've attempted to do. Individuals who are not accepted by the most popular crowd have an inner beauty that can be admired and appreciated. Frequently, I have grown to love and admire these individuals. They've often become my best friends.

Larry was handsome inside and out. Watching and observing Larry and the interactions he had with his peers, I knew that he wasn't necessarily in the popular group but everyone on campus seemed to know him. Something also told me that he had been trampled on many times by his peers in the past; maybe that was part of the tremendous hurt that surfaced inside of him from time to time. But past that hurt, past that pain, past the insecurities, and past other people's beliefs, not everyone saw what my friends and I did. Often the most vulnerable people are the ones who are attacked the most by others. Larry was no exception. But his close friends on campus who truly took the time to become acquainted with him grew to deeply admire and respect him. Inside, he was a wonderful person who cared deeply about others.

I was blessed with the incredible opportunity of becoming well acquainted with Larry. Overlooking all weaknesses was so easy, because I could see that his concern for others was genuine. His care and compassion to meet the needs of others is something that we all can learn from. If anyone expressed a need, Larry was eager to fulfill it. I will never forget the incident that happened as we traveled back to campus following the movie, which perfectly exemplified this quality. We were driving up the bridge that leads to the main street into town, and just as we were climbing up the hill, Larry noticed a car had pulled off on the side of the road. Its hazard lights were flashing, and as soon as Larry noticed it, he suggested we stop and help them out. I pulled my car over to the side of the road, and he quickly jumped out.

A few moments later, Larry returned. "They're out of gas," he said. "Let's go to the gas station up the road and get some gas for them."

The gas station was just half a mile up the road. When we arrived, Larry went inside and asked if he could borrow a gas can. He filled it and paid for it, and we headed back towards the stranded car. After he transferred the gas from the can to their tank, he hopped back in the car. Apparently, they had offered to pay him back for the two dollars' worth of gas, but he refused to take their money. We returned the gas can to the station and headed back to Andrews. Larry truly cared about everyone. Seeing Larry in this situation and how he reacted once again reaffirmed my belief about the quality person he was. Larry didn't just say he cared for others; he showed it. My heart skipped a beat whenever I saw evidence of his generous, caring nature.

~32~

AN ANSWERED PRAYER

One afternoon, I was talking to Lauren, and she shared with me how much Larry had missed me when I was away from Andrews the previous quarter. Larry called her frequently, as he was continually searching for someone to chat with. As spring quarter progressed, Larry and Lauren talked more frequently. The more she became acquainted with him, the more she valued him as a friend. Lauren would often make comments to me about Larry. She remarked on his skill with analogies and words and how he would make an excellent physical therapist because of his caring nature.

Over time, I realized that my friendship with Larry was blossoming into much more. Late one evening as Lauren and I chatted, it finally sunk in just how much Larry meant to me. Lauren made an offhanded comment about how well Larry and I got along. She was right. Larry and I balanced each other out incredibly well. His talkative side balanced out my quietness. His phlegmatic side balanced out my choleric side. And we really bonded over everything.

That evening, I began opening up to her. "Yes, we've always hit it off. He's so talkative, mellow and enthusiastic. I truly admire him."

"I can see the two of you dating," she said. "He likes you just as much as you like him. I see it every time you two are together."

It was then that I remembered my prayer from the previous spring. It was as though the Holy Spirit brought that simple prayer to my attention again. I had forgotten all about it. In my prayer, I had asked God to show me the right person to date. Indeed, I realized, God had answered my prayer. Even though I had begun opening up to Lauren about my feelings for Larry, I still hadn't mentioned anything to Larry. I wanted the Lord to lead with the perfect timing. Indeed, He knew what was best.

One Sabbath afternoon, Lauren and I ate with some of Larry's friends. After eating, we sat and talked for a while before heading down to the lobby of the student center. Larry teased his friends about being engaged.

"The love bug will sting you, too," they retorted.

"Well," Larry replied, "I have an injection for it."

Right! I quietly thought to myself. *Maybe you do, but I sure don't, and I'm positive that an injection would have little effect, especially if I told you three words: I love you!*

~33~

THE MYSTERY BIRD

Larry was supportive of me no matter what crazy things were happening in my life: my distractions, my obsessions, and the crazy assignments my classes required. His unconditional acceptance and support helped my insecurities to vanish. That quarter, even my distraction and interest in the birds outside our dorm room didn't bother him. The birds never seemed to stop making noise and were driving me and my roommate crazy. How could anyone sleep when the racket outside our window was so loud and annoying? A bird was singing the same note for a measure and resting for a few seconds only to begin the same monotonous tune? I liked birds, but those birds were different! They distracted us from our studies and phone conversations. We were desperate to figure out what kinds of birds they were. There was one bird in particular that had a slur at the end of its song. No matter how many times Sophie and I tried to figure out what bird had such a strange song, we never succeeded. It became a joke between us. "There's that bird again," we'd often say, bursting into laughter.

One afternoon when Larry called, we were having a pleasant conversation when my thoughts were interrupted by the slurring bird. I burst out in frustration. "There's that bird again. It's driving me nuts! I wish I knew what kind of bird it was. Can you hear it?" I said lifting the receiver to the window so he could hear. "Do you know what it is?" I asked.

"No," Larry replied. "I don't know very much about birds." If he was laughing at my crazy antics with the birds, he did an excellent job of hiding it. He didn't even comment on how weird I was being. What crazy person would circle around trees searching for a bird that was nowhere in sight?

We never found anybody who could identify the bird, so it remained a mystery to all of us. Fortunately, we survived that quarter without losing our sanity.

34

GRAPE JUICE

One Friday afternoon, I was in the computer lab typing when Larry quietly slipped in and sat down beside me. I was surprised to see him.

"How'd you find out that I was here?" I asked, glancing up at him.

"Sophie told me that you were," he said.

"I'm so glad you came. I need a break," I replied with a sigh as I looked away from the screen and all the work that was in front of me.

He slid a bottle of grape juice over to me. "I thought you might enjoy this," he said.

I thanked him. I was so pleased he had thought about me.

When I later mentioned to Lauren that Larry had given me some grape juice, she told me what Larry had done for her during the previous quarter. They had been talking on the phone, and she shared with him that she was feeling dizzy. He asked if there was anything that helps, and she told him grape juice usually made her feel better.

About thirty minutes later, the receptionist downstairs called Lauren. "A bunch of guys want to see you at West Desk."

When she went down to the desk nobody was there, but a glass of grape juice had been left for her.

"Do you know who left this?" Lauren asked the receptionist.

"It's been a busy afternoon so I don't remember who he was or what he looked like. I do know that it was one man who told me to tell you that a bunch of guys were downstairs."

Later that evening, Lauren called Larry. "Did you give me grape juice today?"

Larry denied doing it and pretended to not know anything about it. "I wonder who it could have been," he replied.

Lauren called Larry again the following morning and thanked him.

"Who told you?" he asked.

"Nobody told me," she said.

"Well, I guess teachers aren't as gullible as I thought," Larry replied.

Larry was constantly thinking about others. He always brightened other people's days and did whatever he could to relieve their stress. Often, Lauren and I talked about Larry and how much we appreciated his care and concern for others. We also saw a side of him that was deeply hurting. He was struggling to accept himself. How could we help him realize just how special he was? He became a part of our prayer list that quarter. We would pray together, asking God to help him. Only the Lord knew exactly what was needed to take away Larry's hurt. And taking away his hurt meant the entire world to me because he was such a special person.

35

A TENNIS DATE

I t seemed like I hardly saw Larry unless I happened to pass him walking on campus. At least I knew I would always see him during assembly on Fridays. I looked forward to seeing Larry and to discussing our weekend plans. He was taking a tennis class that quarter, and every once in a while, he'd mention to me that he needed to practice with someone. One Friday in assembly, I asked him if he'd like to play tennis. Although I'd taken a tennis class the quarter before, it had been several weeks since I had played.

"I can't today, because I'm going to the mall with Emilia this afternoon," Larry replied.

"That's fine," I said.

"How about playing tennis on Sunday?" he asked. "I'll call you so we can set up a time to meet."

"Okay. That sounds good."

I was studying on Sunday when Larry phoned in the early evening. "Do you still want to play tennis?" he asked.

"Sure!" I replied. "I'm ready for a break."

"Give me about ten minutes to walk over to campus," Larry said. "I'll meet you at the tennis courts by Meier and Burman Halls."

The courts were full when we arrived.

"Well," he said, "we could go over to the academy and use their courts."

"That's a good idea. I'd forgotten about their courts," I replied. "Let's drive over there."

Larry teased me about being lazy for suggesting we drive to the other courts, which were within walking distance. Since the sun was setting, I wanted to have more time to play. Larry agreed, so we drove over. Fortunately, all the courts were free when we arrived. I was thankful, as I was really looking forward to playing again.

It seemed like much of our playing time was spent chasing tennis balls. Six balls just didn't seem to be enough. As we got going, though, we improved and spent a little less time chasing and more time hitting balls. Larry kept score, since I had too much difficulty trying to hit the balls and keep score at the same time.

Eventually, we gave up on scoring and just practiced hitting the balls.

"You serve," Larry said. "You're much better at it than I am." So, I'd serve the balls, and we'd practice hitting them back and forth. By the end, we were both improving. We stayed until it was almost dark. Both of us were enjoying ourselves. If the lighting had been better, we probably would have stayed longer.

As we traveled back to campus, Larry informed me of his decision to stay with Emilia's family over summer vacation. Emilia had invited him earlier that quarter, and he had decided to accept the invitation. He would stay with her family and work. I loved Emilia's friendly, supportive, compassionate family. They were talkative, warm, and loving, and they treated any new person who came to stay with them as part of their family. It did sound like a wonderful place for Larry to spend his summer vacation, but I knew that I was desperately going to miss him.

After dropping Larry off and saying goodnight to him, I went to Lauren's room to chat with her. I told her about Larry's plan to spend the summer with Emilia. We prayed about it, petitioning God to work everything out for Larry. We both thanked God for Larry's opportunity to spend the summer with his friends. We knew that everything was in God's hands. He would continue to guide and direct Larry. We also asked that the Lord help Larry learn enough Spanish to communicate with Emilia's family.

At some point during that quarter, my mind recalled the prayer that I had prayed during the previous winter. I'd asked God to send someone to me whom I could minister to. Suddenly, the Holy Spirit revealed that God had indeed answered my prayer. It was as though the Lord had opened my eyes or at least had assisted me with the ability to remember my prayer. God had sent Larry, I realized. Larry was reaching out for friends who would respect him for who he was. I realized that Emilia, Maria, Isabel, Lauren, Sophie, and I had become just some of the friends God guided to Larry, among many others on campus who grew to deeply appreciate him. God planted the desire in Emilia's heart to have Larry live with her family during the summer. Lauren became the one who listened and provided Larry with advice when he needed it.

My role with Larry was entirely unique. I became the one who spent hours talking to him, listening to him, encouraging him, laughing with him, and loving him. I was the one Larry chased after for two years, wondering if his desire to date me would ever come true. What he didn't realize was that spending time together in our informal activities and casual dates was causing me to fall increasingly more in love with him every single day, in every single way.

~36~

TELEPHONE OPERATOR

One Saturday night, I had finally had enough with my phone jack. At the most inopportune moments, especially when I was talking to Larry, it would come out of the wall and disconnect the line. When that happened and Larry was on the line, he'd often tease, "Don't you like talking to me?" I'd been fighting with the phone for most of the year and had finally reached my limit, so I decided to buy a new jack to solve the problem. Sophie and I attempted to cut the wire, but the knife that we had simply wasn't working. I went down to Emilia's room and ran into Julia, who had the brilliant suggestion to cut the cord with scissors. Unfortunately, the new jack still wasn't working, and Emilia pointed out that I had purchased the wrong jack. I was too tired to think any more about it, so I decided to sleep on it.

The next morning, I woke up early to study. Seeing the telephone cord sprawled out on my desk, I came up with an idea. I began peeling the plastic coating off the wires and inserted them into the phone outlet. I picked up the phone and heard a dial tone. *Hurray, it works!* I thought. Now all I needed to do was secure it. A little while later, Sophie woke up and saw what I had been working on. We decided to test it out. I picked up the phone, but it was dead. I undid the tape and moved the wires. Amazingly, the phone rang at that moment. I told Sophie to answer it while I held the wires. It had been Larry, hoping to talk to me, but I'd moved the wires and lost the connection. *Now what?* I thought.

I pushed the wires back into place, and Sophie hung up the phone. As I did that, the phone rang again. This time, it was Rob calling for Sophie. She was able to say hello, but then both of us burst out laughing. When I accidentally moved the wire, the line disconnected. I reattached the wires again, but we had the same luck. Sophie ran downstairs to call Rob. She returned shortly afterward. I connected the wires again and phoned Lauren, but I got to laughing so uncontrollably that I broke the connection. I ran downstairs to tell Lauren about our telephone escapade. I was laughing so hard that I could hardly talk. Lauren motioned for me to be quieter since Camille, her sister, was sleeping. She stepped outside to talk to me.

By that point, I'd calmed down enough to tell her what I'd done. "Could I borrow one of your phones until I can go buy another one?" I asked.

Lauren reached into her room and disconnected a phone. I raced upstairs to plug it in and phoned Larry, but nobody answered. I hoped that Larry would call back.

When I returned, Sophie and I burst into laughter again.

"Boy!" I told Sophie. "I must be the most entertaining roommate that you've ever had. Who would ever think of holding wires into place so they could make a phone call?"

After all of our trouble, I decided that I'd better just buy a new phone, so I went to the store. When I returned, Sophie informed me that Larry had called. "Evidently, he ran in the 5k race," Sophie said. "He asked why you hadn't run in it."

"Well, I'll call him back, now that the phone is working," I said, laughing as I recalled that morning's fiasco. Almost as soon as Larry realized that it was me, he asked the same question he'd asked Sophie.

"Why didn't you run in the 5k race?" he said. "I ran in it, because I thought you'd be there."

"I decided not to this year. I really haven't been running very faithfully, and I still don't have as much energy as I did before I got mono. So, I chose not to this year. I'm sorry."

"Well," he said. "I wish you could have come down to see me this morning."

"I didn't know that you were running in it, or I would have," I replied. "Where did you call from this morning?"

"Nethery Hall," he replied.

"Oh, after you called this morning, I tried to phone you at your apartment. No wonder you weren't there. I'm sorry you couldn't get through this morning, but we were having trouble with our phone." Then I told him "the telephone jack story," as Sophie and I had termed the incident.

"No wonder I couldn't get through!" he teased.

Life with Larry was never dull. He had a unique way of taking life's annoyances and problems and turning them into opportunities to help. Later, I would realize just how important his outlook would mean to me for the remainder of my life.

37

GIFTS

O ne Friday, Lauren and I agreed to meet Larry in Seminary Sabbath School class the following morning. The day dawned with beautiful brilliance. The flowers were beginning to blossom, and birds were singing. The weather was still cool, so I grabbed my jacket and descended the stairs to Lauren's room.

Early Sabbath morning, Larry called. "Do you have gray thread and a needle that I could borrow? I need to sew a button on my suit."

"I think I do," I responded. "Let me check just to make sure. Yes, I do."

"Could you bring it to Sabbath School?"

"Sure," I replied, grabbing the thread, needle, and scissors. I put them inside my purse. The Sabbath school class was full when Lauren and I arrived. On the platform, we suddenly discovered a few vacant seats where we sat next to the teacher. A few minutes later,

Larry arrived. When he spotted Lauren, he sat down beside us.

"Did you bring the thread and needle?" Larry whispered a few minutes later.

"Yes," I replied and carefully hauled them out of my purse.

He took the sewing supplies, threaded the needle, and launched into sewing on the button. I was surprised by his skill. When he finished, he gently tucked the thread back in my purse and began listening even more intently to the discussion. When passages were read, he followed along in my Spanish-English Bible, attempting to read some of the passages in Spanish. Every once in a while, he'd ask me what certain Spanish words meant.

"This is a great way to practice my Spanish," he whispered to me, "but if I can't understand this, how am I ever going to survive at Emilia's home this summer?" he asked.

Before long, the quarter was almost over and exam week was a few days away. It was hard to believe that school would soon be over. Larry called me later that weekend and asked if I would like to go to an amusement park with him and Emilia.

"We're trying to get a group together so we can go," he said. "Would you like to come? This will be the last time that we can get together like this till next school year."

I knew it would be amusing and enjoyable, but the practical side of me said that I couldn't.

"Exam week is just a week away," I replied. "I really need to study. If it fell on a better week, I'd go. I understood that Larry sincerely wanted me to go, and I wanted to spend time with him, but I also knew that I needed to study for exams.

"Enjoy yourself!" I said.

"Oh, don't worry, I will. Now you're making me feel guilty about going."

Sophie departed for a band trip that weekend, so I had the room to myself. With fewer distractions, I should have accomplished oodles of things that weekend, but as sometimes is the case when one has an enormous amount of time on their hands, they often waste it. That was the situation for me that weekend. I was literally losing steam. How would I ever survive exam week if my attention span consisted of no more than five minutes? Prayer was my solitary solution. *"Lord, please help me with my studying,"* I prayed.

Lauren and I consumed countless hours conversing together that weekend. On Friday evening, we chatted in my room into the wee hours of the morning. Finally, we decided that we'd better prepare for bed so we could wake up for church in the morning. Lauren went down to her room. A few minutes later, I heard someone gently rapping on my door. I was surprised to discover Lauren standing there when I opened the door.

"What happened?" I asked.

"My sister apparently invited someone to spend the night, and they were sound asleep when I entered the room," Lauren replied. "Do you mind if I sleep here tonight? I don't want to disturb them."

"That's fine," I said. "You can sleep on the top bunk since Sophie isn't here."

Lauren slept in my room for the remainder of that weekend. It was wonderful, because it provided an opportunity for us to chat together. More importantly, it provided us with motivation to study. On Saturday night, we decided to wake up early the next morning to study. Our plan seemed like a good one, since we both required a partner to study with so we'd be more motivated, but neither of us could sleep. It wasn't often that either of us had an opportunity to talk like this.

"Let's get up and study," I suggested. "We might as well since we can't sleep."

We turned on the light and plopped down at the desk to study. No more than ten seconds passed before I heard Lauren ask, "Are you hungry?"

"No, are you? If so, I have some fruit," I said pointing at the stack of ripe bananas.

Neither of us really thought they looked particularly appetizing, but we both decided to eat one. We went back to studying, but soon I burst out laughing and Lauren soon joined in.

"This is useless," I said. "I'm going out to the lobby to study."

Fifteen minutes passed, and then Lauren appeared in the doorway to see how I was doing.

"Are you tired?" she asked when she saw my eyelids drooping and my head nodding. A huge smile spread across her face and we both laughed, deciding it was time to go to sleep. We crawled back into bed and quickly drifted off to sleep. We awoke late the next morning, fixed breakfast, and began studying. This time, our efforts paid off. Finally, we were getting somewhere. Sometimes we would digress into long periods of conversation, and an hour would elapse before we knew it. To help with this, we came up with a system that worked extremely well. When we decided we had chatted for long enough, one of us would yell, "One, two, three, stop!" It was our signal to stop talking on the count of three. That usually was effective, but sometimes it led to me laughing every time I'd glance at her. A barricade became a necessity so neither of us would stare at each other and begin giggling. Neither Lauren nor I managed to sleep much that weekend, but by the time Monday night arrived, we could both seriously declare that we had studied.

On Monday evening, I was exhausted and weary from studying so I decided to go running. I bumped into Emilia and Larry on the way back to my dorm. They had just returned from the amusement park in Chicago. Larry informed me that he won two stuffed animals.

"That's great," I replied. "It's hard to win anything at those booths. I always end up wasting my money." I could tell though that he was disappointed.

"I was hoping to win a huge stuffed animal," he said. "Instead, I won some dinky ones. Emilia has them in her room. There is one for you and one for Lauren, since neither of you could come along."

"Thanks," I answered. "That was very thoughtful of you."

"I'll give them to you later," Emilia replied.

When I finally received the stuffed animals, I showed them to Lauren. We both burst into boisterous laughter. They were comical looking. No wonder Larry wasn't impressed. Even if he hadn't been enthralled by them, they genuinely brightened our day.

The week elapsed much the same as the weekend had, as Lauren stayed in my room most nights.

"It's nice," I told Lauren. "It's like old times when we used to study together in Spain."

All of us benefitted. We were all struggling to study, especially since the weather was so brilliantly sunny and gorgeous. We would have given anything to enjoy the outdoors, but summer vacation would soon arrive. That seemed to be our only hope. The laughter and entertainment of studying together also helped. I'd been considering enrolling in classes that summer so I could finish all of my bachelor's degree courses in December. I was beginning to question the wisdom of studying in the summer, though, because of all the difficulty that I was having that week.

"I don't want to stay here this summer," I complained to Lauren and Sophie. "I'm worn out. I really need a break. If I'm this bad now, how will I ever study this summer? I'm a nervous breakdown waiting to happen."

"Maybe you can come home with me this summer," Lauren said. "It would sure be nice to spend the summer with you."

Lauren called her grandmother and asked her to inquire about places I might be able to work if I were to stay with them over the summer. Unfortunately, I wasn't able to find any work, so it looked like I would have to stay at Andrews for the summer.

"I know God has a reason for wanting you to stay here this summer," Lauren reassured me. "Maybe He sees the importance of you completing some courses this summer so you can graduate in December."

I knew she was right. I had to trust God's wisdom. I didn't know why; all I knew was I couldn't see into the future like God could. I just had to trust. God knew what was best. Now, in retrospect, I am incredibly grateful that I completed my coursework in December. Indeed, God did know what was best. If only I could have seen into the future like God could.

38

A SURPRISE BIRTHDAY PARTY

That weekend was Larry's birthday, and my friends and I decided to prepare something special for him. Lauren and I had driven to the store the previous week to purchase something for Larry. After searching for a while, we finally bought a plaid green and purple shirt. We hoped that it would be big enough. Once we'd gotten the shirt, we started planning more of the details about the party. Eventually, we settled on the location. The next issue to decide was how to coerce Larry to come to my grandmother's house without causing any suspicion.

On Friday afternoon, I drove over to my grandmother's house to bake the cake. Finally, the last preparations had been accomplished, and I was ready to meet Lauren and Sophie. We chatted for a while and Lauren informed me of the plan that she had devised to persuade Larry to come over to my grandmother's house. Then we called Emilia and told her about our plan. They would bike over to my grandmother's house and wait there while Lauren, Sophie, and I lured Larry out for a walk. When we were about to meet Larry for our walk, Lauren realized she had left her laundry in the washing machine. Larry, Sophie, and I sat on the sculpture outside the science complex and talked while we waited for Lauren. Then we brought up our idea to Larry.

"What would you like to do tonight?" Lauren asked.

"I don't know," Larry replied.

"Why don't we have vespers?" I suggested. "We can go over to my grandmother's house, sing, and have our own worship service.

"That sounds like a good idea," Lauren said. "I can take my guitar. I'll go up and get it and meet you guys out in front."

Lauren returned a few minutes later with her guitar, and we loaded it in the trunk of my car. Then we traveled over to my grandmother's apartment.

"It looks like it's going to rain," I said as we climbed out of my car. I sure hoped that everyone would make it back on their bikes before it started pouring. Thankfully, Larry didn't seem suspicious. My grandmother met us at the door. As we walked in, everyone inside yelled

"Surprise!" Larry had a shocked look on his face as he turned to Lauren, Sophie, and me. "That was a sneaky way to get me over here."

"Yeah, it was," I said. "But it worked, didn't it?" He just smiled.

I talked to my grandmother for a few minutes and helped her place the cake and a few other items on the table. We sang "Happy Birthday" to Larry and then served the cake. We talked for a little while and then presented Larry with his package and some cards.

"What's in this?" he asked, pointing to the package.

"You'll have to open it and find out," Lauren replied.

He opened it and held the shirt up to examine it. "I really like it," he said.

"Why don't you try it on?" Lauren suggested. "We don't know if it's the right size, but if it isn't you can exchange it."

He slipped into the bathroom to pull it on and stepped out in the hallway to examine it.

"I really like it," he said. "It feels okay, but it's a little tight in the armpits."

"Well, let us know if you want to exchange it. We still have the receipt," Lauren answered.

"Oh, that's okay, I'll keep it. If it gets too tight, I'll frame it. You guys sure are sneaky. I guess I'll have to watch you more closely next time."

The next day, I woke up early to prepare for church. The phone rang, and I answered it. Larry's voice came through the receiver.

"Are you going to Spanish church today?" he asked.

"Well, I was planning on going to a different service, but I really don't have a preference," I replied.

"Emilia invited me to go to Spanish church with her," Larry said. Would you like to go, too?"

"Sure, that's fine. I'll just give Lauren a call and tell her that I'm going to the Spanish church." About twenty minutes later, I curled back up on my bed to rest for a few minutes. I was exhausted. I would have loved to just go to sleep, but I knew that I couldn't really afford to take a nap. A few minutes after I'd laid down, the phone rang. It was Larry again.

"Emilia still hasn't come to get me," he said. "Can you come and pick me up? I think she may have forgotten about me."

"Sure! Just give me about ten minutes. I'm still not quite ready. I fell asleep again."

"Okay," Larry replied. "I'll just start walking over."

By the time I'd finished getting ready and had gotten in my car to meet Larry, he'd already walked from his apartment to the university apartments. It was raining and overcast that morning. I was amazed to see Larry walking outside without an umbrella.

"Didn't you bring an umbrella?" I asked as he climbed in the car.

"No. I got outside and saw the weather, but I didn't want to go back and get one. I just hoped that it wouldn't start raining too hard before you arrived."

I apologized that it had taken me so long. I really hadn't expected him to walk so far, especially in the rain. It was so like Larry to be considerate of me and my feelings. Getting soaked didn't even seem to bother him. His only concern was my welfare. His selflessness had become an essential part of my life, a part I never wanted to let go.

39

SURPRISES

The pressures of the quarter culminated with the traditional, stressful final examinations. All of us were stressed and worried about the material we were required to remember. So, to help us all survive the pressures of that week, Lauren camped out in our room. She was as overwhelmed as Sophie and I. Focusing on studying was difficult, especially with the onset of the sunny spring weather. We formed a study trio, encouraging each other in our efforts. We'd join hands and pray together before scampering off to face our exams. When we returned, we'd share the outcome with each other and shout for joy that another exam had been completed.

One evening, Lauren and I decided that we needed a change of scenery, so we went down to the first-floor lobby to study. I'd forgotten some notes and dashed back to my room to retrieve them. When I entered my dorm, Sophie informed me that a package had been left for me.

"It's there on your desk," Sophie said, pointing to it.

"Do you know who it's from?" I asked looking in the direction she was pointing while moving toward my desk.

"There wasn't a note attached to it, but I'd assume it was from Larry."

I hastily opened it. Inside, I found a piece of cantaloupe.

"It has to be Larry," I said noticing there was no note. "Who else could it be? That's really nice of him."

I went back down to study and told Lauren about my gift.

"I think Camille mentioned something earlier about a package being left for me," Lauren told me as she raced off to look. A few minutes later, Lauren returned with the cantaloupe in hand and a huge smile on her face. We were both grateful for the unexpected gifts. Later that week, I was cramming for an exam when Larry phoned. I was extremely stressed out and was beginning to feel that it was all hopeless. Larry recognized instantly that I was anxious and worried about my test, so he kept our conversation brief and shared words of encouragement before hanging up. "I'm sure you'll do fine," he said.

Larry's reassurance and Lauren's and Sophie's support pulled me through exam week. We all gathered together and prayed before I left for my final exams. By the grace of God we all passed our tests. Finally, we were free. Summer vacation had arrived and everyone was preparing to travel home. Rooms quickly emptied, and soon there would be almost no one left on campus.

When my exams were finally over, I received a phone call from Larry as he prepared for his departure, "Would you like to use my computer this summer?" he asked. "I don't have room to take it with me. If you'd like, you can use it."

"Sure, I don't have a computer so I'd be grateful to use yours this summer."

"I'll bring it over for you," Larry promised.

"Okay, great. Thanks! It really will be a blessing," I said thinking about my summer term papers.

"Will I get to see you before you leave?" he asked with sadness in his voice.

"I'll come over before I leave tomorrow morning." We set a time to meet before hanging up.

"Awesome! I'll see you then," he said

After lugging everything to my car early the next morning, I raced up to Emilia's room to tell her goodbye. Afterwards, I strolled over to Lauren's room and we prayed together before I left.

I climbed into my car and drove to Larry's apartment, anxiously hoping that he was awake. He greeted me at the door when I arrived and we unhurriedly walked to my car. We lingered near my car talking, aching for the moment to last as long as possible. The heaviness of another goodbye hung in the air.

"I hope you have a good summer," I told Larry while we embraced. As he firmly clutched me in his arms, I ached to express to him just how much I loved him. He held me for as long as he could and then he stood in the yard waving to me as I slowly drove away. I prayed that he'd have a wonderful time at Emilia's house. As I thought about how much I would miss him, tears flowed from my eyes. The thought of not being with Larry filled my heart with loneliness. I just never could have imagined what it would be like not to have Larry with me. Little did I know that the time was coming when I wouldn't have Larry in my life anymore, and I would find out exactly what that felt like.

~40~

CAMILLE

Driving home, my mind was consumed by thoughts of Larry. I prayed his summer vacation would be awesome. Larry would be in excellent hands. Everyone in Emilia's family had loving spirits, nurturing hearts, and hospitable natures that would be wonderful for Larry. Speaking Spanish would be a challenge, but immersion is always the best way to learn a language.

The summer did not entice me in the least. Studying for classes was not a pleasant thought. Motivating myself to study would be difficult. My only encouragement and motivation came from the fact that I was one quarter away from graduating. Finally, my bachelor's degree was in sight. The other gratifying reflection was my closeness to the beaches. The departure of my friends, though, was difficult. Goodbyes were always hard. The few faces that remained sustained me. Isabel and Camille were staying for the summer, so I wouldn't be left totally alone.

After a short vacation at home, I traveled back to Andrews. I discovered a note in my dorm room that read: "Please move to your assigned summer dormitory room as soon as possible." I was dreading the moving process, but fortunately my new room was close by and I was sharing it with Camille. When I opened the door to my new room, I was shocked by the sight of mounds of clothes and an incredible array of items, boxes, suitcases, books, and clutter. There was no room for my belongings. Abruptly, I slammed the door shut. The disaster was too much to consider wading through.

Okay, now what? I thought. Tackling the mess was too much think about, so I decided to talk to Lauren, since she was Camille's sister and could help me. I found her in the computer lab, and she warned me that she'd had to move her belongings into the room along with Camille's. Her car was having problems, so she was having to stay on campus longer than expected. After our conversation, we didn't lose much time. With all of my belongings having to be moved by that evening, we scurried over to the dorm. Within two days, everything was neatly organized and all of Lauren's belongings were in storage. Even though the task was exhausting, it was wonderful to spend time with Lauren. We had an excellent time talking in spite of the grueling and demanding work. It provided us with many hours to discuss our summer plans and to pray together. We knew God was in control of everything, although we still longed to spend the summer together. For some reason, though, God's plans prevented it. The unopened doors continued pointing to my need to study at Andrews that summer.

Lauren's car situation delayed her summer employment by a week, which meant that she could attend my cousin's wedding with me. Also, she'd have the opportunity to meet my family, and maybe we could convince my grandfather, a respectable carpenter, to make supports for the loft we had in our room.

The day of the wedding arrived, bringing brilliant sunlight, crystal blue skies, and perfect balmy weather. We silently settled down to enjoy the service. It was delightful to observe the decorations, listen to the music, and watch the ceremony. The entire service commenced on a positive note, and everything was going as planned. When the final music selection was played, a hush spread over the audience and serious, somber expressions lined everyone's faces. Suddenly, the solemn silence was broken by chuckles and hearty laughter escaping from the audience. We surveyed what was happening. Then we noticed the backsides of my cousin and his wife kneeling on the ground. Everything initially appeared fine until our eyes fell on the soles of my cousin's enormous shoes, where two words were written: "Help Me!" By the end of the ceremony, everyone was laughing and smiling.

When we were ushered to exit the church, we were directed to Chan Shun Hall for the reception. Everything was elegantly decorated. Brilliant balloons hung from the ceiling, and a gorgeous table displayed mints, nuts, and other finger foods. It was a simple and short reception, but it was very stylish. Within forty-five minutes, the cake was carefully cut and served. Finally, the throwing of the bouquet was announced. All the eligible ladies made their way toward the bride. Lauren and I marched over together. When the bouquet was thrown, it sailed straight towards my open hands, and I easily caught it. I could hardly believe it. Whether the significance behind the bouquet toss was true or not, I knew that only time would tell. Everything was in God's hands. If He desired for me and Larry to start dating, I knew that He would ultimately lead. God indeed was in control of everything.

I hung the bouquet of gorgeous pink Peruvian lilies on the post of our loft when we returned to the dormitory. Lauren and I chatted for a while about the wedding and the bouquet. We also talked about Larry, hoping and praying that everything was going well for him. She knew that I admired him and that I was going to miss him.

Before Lauren left for the summer, we phoned Larry, anxious to learn how he was doing. It was wonderful to hear his voice again! He sounded like he was doing well and seemed excited and pleased with the way things were working out.

"The only thing that I don't like is that there's too much concrete. I miss the grass and trees, but Emilia thinks I'll have lots of job opportunities here. I've already submitted applications for several jobs, but I'm waiting to hear from them."

We knew he was adjusting to life in an enormous city, but as always, he was truthfully enjoying himself. Emilia's family really treasured having Larry there that summer as well. They encouraged him, loved him, and nurtured him. He became like family to them. All of Emilia's nieces and nephews also loved playing with Larry.

"Emilia's parents speak mostly Spanish to me, but fortunately they know a few English words. If I really get stumped with their Spanish, they try to explain it in English. I'm slowly picking up more words.

Fortunately, Emilia and her brother know English, so they can help me out when I get stuck. This is giving me a great opportunity to learn Spanish."

Sometimes it was difficult to hear Larry on the phone, because there was always a lot of talking and commotion in the background. Emilia's home was always bustling with people and activities. Everyone who entered their home was welcomed and put at ease. They enjoyed fellowshipping with others, and they had an extremely close-knit family. Larry became part of their family instantly. Everyone treated him as though he were a long lost relative. Daily, they encouraged Larry, expressed only positive words, shared their joy and enthusiasm at having him stay at their house, and imparted love, admiration, and praise to him. The impact of this positive relationship was a tremendous boost in his confidence and self-esteem. It was just the experience Larry needed. The warm affection of Emilia's family softened and erased the negative words Larry had heard from former peers and past experiences. Finally, Larry was hearing the positive, kind, compassionate encouragement all of us need to hear. The care that Emilia's family provided caused Larry to grow spiritually, as well. He was experiencing the love that God has for each of us. I could see that it was helping him grow in his relationship with God.

Finally, the time of Lauren's departure arrived. I truly enjoyed the extra time we'd shared and would miss her tremendously. But we promised to keep in touch.

My classes would begin the following week, and I registered for three courses: junior English, junior communications, and a practicum in audiology. In order to begin my audiology practicum, I needed to prove that I remembered how to utilize the audiometer for hearing evaluations. Before I assessed a client's hearing, I had to perform an evaluation on someone. So, I decided to ask my grandfather if I could test his hearing. My skills were rusty at first, but thankfully my professor walked me through the process. Patiently, my grandfather waited for me to complete the testing. I was pleased that he provided me with the opportunity to practice my skills! It really helped refresh the information that I had learned the previous year.

Slowly, the quarter commenced. I decided on a topic for the research paper I was expected to write on something related to my field of study, speech-language pathology and audiology. As I researched different possibilities, I narrowed down my choices and finally decided to write about hearing impairment and the importance of early intervention in children.

Gradually, I developed a routine study schedule. I had English and communications first thing in the morning, and my audiology practicum was two afternoons a week. I spent my free afternoons researching in the library. In the early evenings, I exercised. My rigorous fitness program was altered when I contracted mono. I knew that I'd have to condition myself again before I could attempt to run the distance that I had been accustomed to running. Although I'd walked a few times without friends, it was no fun and I was frustrated by the slow pace so I decided to ride my bicycle instead. After my first ride around campus, the thrill of the sport filled me with enthusiasm. It became my exercise of choice that summer. I enjoyed the cool breeze that hit my face as I pedaled along and especially liked exploring the neighborhoods behind campus. Frequently, I rode around the neighborhood where Larry's apartment was, wishing and aching to see him. Cycling around near his apartment reminded me of his presence and somehow made me feel closer to him. I missed him terribly. My heart longed to be with him again. He would have made the bicycle rides even more enjoyable. If Larry had been with me to ride bikes together, it wouldn't have felt like exercise. It would have been a fun and happy time that we could have enjoyed together just like we always did with everything else. Being together was all that really mattered to me.

~41~

A SPECIAL FAMILY

C amille continued the difficult task of studying for the intensive physics course that she was enrolled in that summer. She was kept extremely busy with studying and completing her assignments. It was a grueling course. I continued to pray that the Lord would help Camille pass the class. When she finished the final test, she breathed a sigh of relief. She was looking forward to working at a local care home for the elderly and socializing again.

That summer, Camille introduced me to the Johnson family. While Larry was surrounded by a loving nurturing family, God also provided me with an excellent model of what God intended families to be like. Divorce has shattered my family in so many ways, so this vision was something I also needed to see. It was this experience that God used to light my way. At the Johnson's home, I felt welcomed and could sense the closeness of the family. I grew to admire their firm

Christian focus and love for God. Happiness radiated from their faces. I enjoyed the Friday evening or Sabbath afternoon vespers we had at their home. It was wonderful to sing and read together from the Bible. I admired the warmth and affection that came from their hearts. It helped me witness the positive aspects that God wishes to endow to all families. Truly, their home mirrored this vision: "The home that is beautified by love, sympathy, and tenderness is a place that Angels love to visit, and where God is glorified. The Christian home is to be an object lesson, illustrating the excellence of the true principles of life. Such an illustration will be a power for good in the world."[4]

I experienced this as I grew to know the Johnson family that summer. They provided an excellent model of the happiness and pleasure that abound from a close, God-centered family. It was their love, care, and joy that served to light my way. It reminded me of the true vision God has for families. This special memory will remain with me forever.

42

LETTERS

Despite the fact that most of my friends had traveled home for the summer, I continued to communicate with them either by phone or through letters. Lauren's summer was consumed by work at a paint factory near her grandparent's home where she was living. She was thrilled to see her family again, but both of us tremendously missed each other. Almost every weekend, we called to catch up on how things were going. Both of us really appreciated our conversations. They provided us with encouragement and the assurance that the Lord would help us face the challenges that the new week would bring. Sometimes Lauren would call Larry to find out how things were going. Anything she learned about Larry she'd willingly share with me. I also phoned Larry several times that summer. Lauren and I were always encouraged by his cheerful, enthusiastic responses and obvious pleasure about his summer adventures.

"I'm working for a sports club," he told me enthusiastically in one of our conversations. "My job is to monitor and make sure people don't stay in the sauna for too long. I like my job, and I'm pleased to be earning money."

Our conversations were often about places that he'd visited with Emilia and her family. Sometimes he'd tell me about Emilia's nieces and nephews. He always sounded optimistic. I was thrilled that his summer was going so well, but our conversations only partly removed and softened the intense yearning I had to be closer to him. I really missed him. I longed for the remaining weeks of the summer to pass quickly so I could see him again. Hardly a moment passed by that summer when I wasn't thinking and dreaming about him.

Summer quarter drew to a close. My research paper was finally written, and my presentation was finished. Only a month remained until fall quarter would begin. Camille decided to move off campus following the completion of summer quarter, and I traveled home so I could work for the remainder of the summer. I was thankful that only a month remained until the start of fall quarter. I longed to see Larry again. My heart was breaking. I felt like I would explode.

The summer ended on a sad note when my cat became ill. My parents rushed him to an emergency veterinarian, who informed us that my cat was extremely sick and there was little hope for improvement in his condition. We decided to have him put to sleep. It was a depressing moment for all of us. His absence was magnified by the intense silence that enveloped our home. I was thankful that I'd soon be returning to Andrews so I could be distracted from the pain of missing my cat.

Before returning to Andrews that fall, I felt an intense conviction to write to Larry. I had written to him multiple times that summer, but I knew in my heart that it was time to express my deepest feelings to him. It was as if the lid that had kept my emotions bottled up for so long was finally removed. I could not suppress my feelings any longer. I deeply cared for Larry, and I had to tell him how much I loved him. If writing a letter would make the difference so that Larry would know—really know—how I felt, then that was the very least I could do. And maybe, just maybe, this letter would be the beginning of a brand-new horizon and life for the two of us.

43

FRIENDSHIP BLOSSOMS

Returning to Andrews that fall quarter was wonderful. I phoned Emilia immediately and learned that they had returned a few days before. Larry had gone home to spend the weekend with his family, but he would be returning that evening. Emilia promised that she would tell Larry I had called. I couldn't wait to see him! The hours ticked by slowly. It seemed like an eternity. The afternoon turned into evening, and still I had not heard from Larry. When would he return? I grew gloomier as the evening progressed. How much longer could I wait? I felt as if I would explode. Lauren could see my downcast spirit, and she tried to encourage me.

Our conversation was soon interrupted by the ringing phone. Lauren answered it and told me it was Larry. He was waiting in West Lobby. As much as I ached to see him, another part of me was incredibly nervous. My heart started racing, and I could feel my face suddenly flush. Lauren could see that my anxiety level was intensifying.

"Let's pray together before you go down," she told me. "Remember, it's all in God's hands." Then she shared some Bible texts with me and prayed that God would calm me and give me the right words. As Lauren was saying the closing words to her prayer, the phone rang again. It was Larry wondering if we were coming. Obviously, he must have been impatient and anxious as well. He asked Lauren to come down, too.

After Lauren replaced the receiver in the cradle, she gave me a hug. "I'll be praying for you," she told me. "I'll stay up until you return." Together, we descended the stairs and were soon greeted by Larry's cheerful voice. A surprised expression spread over Larry's face when he noticed me. He almost didn't recognize me.

"What happened to your hair?" he asked.

All my nervousness melted away when I saw him. "I got it cut short," I said, smiling and noticing that he, too, had a shorter haircut.

"Yeah, but I didn't expect it to be that short!" he said in surprise.

The summer had brought changes to him as well. He seemed happier and more self-confident. His typical enthusiasm was present but he had matured and seemed more secure in himself. Lauren said hi to Larry and hastily departed, knowing that Larry and I were anxious to be alone. He and I started strolling around with no destination in mind. Eventually, we found ourselves in front of Meier Hall, where my brother was living having just started his freshman year.

"Why don't you call your brother?" Larry suggested. "I'd like to meet him."

We went into Meier, and I called my brother from the lobby phone. Nobody answered, so we headed back outside. Soon we were met by a heavy torrent of rain.

"Let's find some shelter," Larry said.

We headed to the closest building, which was the student center, and waited in the entryway across from Lamson Hall. The rain didn't appear to be lessening.

"I'll go and get a couple of umbrellas," I told Larry. After all, it was only a few feet to the women's dormitory. As I was racing out of Lamson Hall, I passed Emilia in the lobby and told her that Larry had returned. She asked me to tell him that she wanted to talk with him. I grabbed the umbrellas and rejoined Larry outside. Just as we were preparing to leave, my brother appeared. I introduced him to Larry, and we chatted for a few minutes. Emilia was waiting in front of Lamson Hall, so Larry and I headed that way to talk to her. All of us stood out in the rain chatting. It was wonderful to talk to her again, but I was growing restless and antsy. I fervently wanted to talk with Larry alone. Eventually, Emilia left, and Larry and I trotted off, hoping not to run into anyone else. We darted over to the library and proceeded inside the main entryway to escape from the rain. We sat down on some makeshift benches and chatted.

"I tried to reach you at home. I felt bad about how I ended things in our last conversation. I wanted to apologize," Larry said.

"Oh, don't worry," I replied.

"I spent two years chasing after you," Larry said gleaming at me. "I can't believe I finally got you. I know one of the reasons you were hesitant about dating me was because of what Robin said. Do you still have any doubts?"

"No, of course not," I told him. "I'm sorry. I just needed to be sure."

"I know," Larry said. "But, still, if Robin hadn't said what she said to you, I wouldn't be repeating statistics class this quarter. I failed that class because of you," he said, teasing me. "I wouldn't have had to pursue you for the past two years either."

"I know. I'm sorry. Thank you for being so patient with me."

He smiled back at me. "It's okay, because now I have you," Larry said. He was quiet for a few minutes as he stared into my eyes. "Thank you for sending me that letter. I tried to call you, but your dad got mad at me for calling so late."

"Yeah, I know he told me. I was already in bed when you called. I'm sorry about that."

"How long have you felt that way about me?" he asked

"Since the end of spring semester. Before you left for the summer," I said.

"Why didn't you tell me sooner?"

"Because I wanted you to have a good summer with Emilia and her family. I knew you needed that."

"I would have stayed here with you," he said.

"I know."

"I had a good summer," he said with a huge grin on his face. Even his eyes were smiling.

"I'm so glad," I replied glancing into his sparkling eyes.

Time passed quickly as I learned about the adventures Larry had in the city. He had truly enjoyed himself. Being at Emilia's home that summer had been a blessing for him.

"Remember that game of Pictionary?" Larry finally asked.

"Yes," I said smiling. "How could I ever forget?"

"Remember when you were too shy to hug me at the church service in Burman Hall?"

"Yes," I said.

"I knew at that church service that you were shy and uncomfortable with hugs, and I didn't want to embarrass you by kissing you during the Pictionary game. I'm thankful I responded the way I did, even if everyone laughed at me," he said staring at me intently. "I didn't want to make you uncomfortable."

"Thank you," I replied with even deeper appreciation for Larry.

We sat in silence for a time. Then Larry gently took my hands in his, and we looked lovingly into each other's eyes.

"Why don't we go outside again?" Larry finally said.

It was still sprinkling, so we opened our umbrellas. After a two-year friendship, Larry and I had learned to read each other's expressions. Sometimes we didn't have to talk to convey our thoughts. We walked in silence for a few moments in the rain enjoying the peace and beauty of the early morning. The sky was a brilliant blue, lightened by the spectacular beauty of a full moon.

"Do you still feel the same?" Larry asked, breaking the silence.

"Yes!" I said without hesitation.

For the first time, he was at a loss for words. He silently assisted me with closing my umbrella and made sure I was underneath his so I didn't get wet from the rain. Then he tenderly positioned his arm around my waist and gently pulled me close against his side.

"How does this feel?" I heard him say. "Is this okay?"

"Yes!" I said as a smile spread across my face. It felt so perfect, but then it always had when I was with him. Something had always drawn us together. Larry turned me around and guided us back to the library. We sat down again, embracing as our lips touched. Finally, the time had come to express our love for one another. It could no longer be held back. On September 26th, our friendship blossomed into a new and beautiful relationship, one that I would never regret.

~44~

LARRY'S GIFTS

My final quarter at Andrews started on a note of intense happiness. Larry and I were finally dating, and it was my final semester before graduating. Nothing could discourage me. Each day was so full of surprises. It was a pleasure to wake up each day, because I never knew what the day would bring. The spontaneity and joy of love filled every moment of my day. I couldn't have been happier. I delighted in every minute of my day. Any time I shared with Larry was precious. The bliss and enthusiasm of finally being together softened the perception of our differences. All that mattered was that we loved each other. Love was the magnet that drew us together with such a strong bond that nothing could separate us.

We often ate together in the boisterous, swarming cafeteria. My friends repeatedly commented that they noticed me more than they ever had in the past. I was no longer holed up in my room studying, and they were pleased to discover that change in me. Larry had always been much more outgoing and adventurous than me. He had no difficulty talking to total strangers. His friendliness and talkative nature balanced my quieter side. With Larry's help, I was becoming less shy and reserved.

Larry and I officially began dating on September 26th. Larry was unusual in that he was one to remember details. Some men easily forget about dates or details, but Larry consciously tucked them away in his memory. Even when my birthday was two months away, he was already planning my gifts and talking about how special a day it would be. He made a conscientious effort to add happiness to my days. Just simply spending time together was enough, but even with that knowledge, Larry frequently went out of his way to do special things for me.

One morning shortly after Larry and I started dating, I went to church after class thinking that we had chapel, but nobody was there. Someone told me there wasn't any chapel that day, so I returned to my room, thankful for a break. I had just unlocked my door and entered my room when my eyes fell on the most gorgeous bouquet of red roses in a vase on my desk. I was so surprised! Of course, I knew they were from

Larry, but what I didn't know was how they arrived on my desk. Someone had placed them there, but I didn't know who. Nobody was around when I arrived in the room, not even my suitemates. It puzzled me, and when I asked Larry about it, he refused to tell me his secret. The beautiful roses truly brightened my day, and I was incredibly thankful for Larry's thoughtfulness.

Larry continued to provide excitement for me. He was constantly surprising me with something new. I'll never forget one of the first chapel services Larry and I attended that autumn. Larry always met me at the entryway of the church, and we would sit on the far left-hand aisle. He was one of the designated individuals who distributed attendance cards at the beginning of the service, so he had an assigned aisle that he was required to work. Lauren joined us that day. As I sat down, I noticed Larry whispering something to Lauren. A few seconds later, he gently heaved something out of his backpack and presented me with an attractive orange stuffed cat. The words on its chest said, "Squeeze Me." Larry whispered, "You said you wanted a cat." I laughed, remembering that I had told him how much I missed my cat that had passed away over the summer.

He told me to press the button, which let out shrill, piercing meows. Students in the surrounding pews twisted around to see where the noise was coming from. My face reddened to a bright shade of crimson. Larry covered the cat with his denim jacket to dampen the sounds. We breathed a sigh of relief when the noises finally stopped. I kept the cat on my bed for the rest of the quarter, and it would occasionally cry out in its familiar meow. Sophie and I would laugh every time. It continued to provide many happy moments, and hardly a night passed when the cat wasn't curled up under the covers beside me.

As the quarter progressed, Larry and I slipped into a routine. I had accepted a job working as a desk receptionist from 4 AM to 8 AM. The early hours didn't bother me, since I was a morning person. Larry asked me to call him at 6 AM every morning to wake him up for his 7 AM class, so we would talk for a few minutes each morning. Following work, I would head over to my racquetball class in the gym and then to my chemistry class in the science complex. Larry always waited for me, since my class was in the same room as his. We would catch each other and chat for a few minutes before our next classes began. After our morning classes ended, Larry would walk me back to the dorm. Around noon, I'd meet Larry for lunch, and we'd stroll over to the cafeteria.

Our lunches were never rushed. We would chat for at least an hour before parting ways, and then I'd return to my room to study. During that first week of classes that quarter, neither of us accomplished much in the way of studies. My schedule was more relaxed in the afternoon that first week, because my clinical training wouldn't begin until the following week. Since the pressure of school was less strenuous that first week, I agreed to walks outside in the gorgeous autumn weather. Neither of us were eager to study. Focusing was impossible. We just ached to be together. It was so pleasant to spend time together again.

Because Larry and I were together so much of the time, I was rarely in my room that quarter. I only occasionally spoke with Sophie or Lauren, and usually that was just when I raced up to my room to grab something while Larry patiently waited for me in the lobby. He became accustomed to my "short" runs as they frequently stretched into ten-minute periods when I would talk to my friends. The buzzing phone would remind me that Larry was waiting.

Larry and I spent as much time as possible together. We even began studying together in the library. I'll never forget the first time we studied together. Sitting down, I opened my bag and pulled out my books. Larry opened one of his textbooks, too. After a few minutes of studying, Larry glanced up and launched into a conversation. Then we again returned to our studies. A few minutes later, Larry got up and came back carrying a massive unabridged dictionary.

"Look at this!" he commented, smiling. Then he left to return the humongous book. Again, Larry attempted to study, but I could tell that he was having incredible difficulty concentrating. Every few minutes, his head popped up and he'd ask me a question. Then, finally giving up entirely on focusing, he closed his book and ripped out a sheet of notebook paper.

"I'm going to write you a note," he said. "I want to get into the habit of writing to you, so it won't be as difficult when you're gone next quarter."

While I studied for another half hour, Larry wrote me a note. I wondered when Larry did his homework and whether he always had difficulty concentrating when he studied. Something told me that he did. He was so active! He did enough homework to pass his classes, but I wondered if he had the study habits to pass the rigorous physical therapy program. I knew that he had the intelligence to complete the program and that he would excel at the practical side of the program, but the academics would be a challenge for him. I knew it would be such a disappointment if he wasn't accepted. All I could do was continue to pray for him.

During that quarter, Larry frequently spoke Spanish with me. Being immersed in a Spanish-speaking home, he had acquired a lot of Spanish over the summer. He could express his thoughts verbally and understood the majority of what I said in Spanish.

When I taught him new words, I would sometimes accidentally utilize my Castilian dialect that I'd learned in Spain. He'd repeat my accent and then realize his mistake. It became a joke between us. When I laughed, he realized that he'd copied my accent and he would tease me about my dialect.

"You lisp when you speak Spanish," he would say.

"Don't worry, you'll learn how as well. I can teach you," I'd reply smiling.

He'd then laugh and tell me that he preferred Emilia's accent. I was pleased that his Spanish abilities had improved as much as they had. We both enjoyed practicing our Spanish together. Larry began requesting to attend Spanish church more often.

The first Sabbath that we went to Spanish church, Lauren came with her brother and his friend Jeff, who had recently returned from a year of studying in Germany. I knew that Lauren was excited Jeff was back again that school year, but it appeared that there was more excitement and enthusiasm about his return than Lauren wished to convey. Her eyes sparkled when she was with him. Larry silently whispered, "They'd make a good couple. Look, Lauren's leaning in towards him." Indeed, Lauren had a radiant expression. It certainly did appear that they would make an excellent couple. Was something in the making? Only time would show evidence of what God had planned.

~45~

FLORAL SURPRISE

That quarter, I registered for an introductory floral arranging course. I was excited about the class, because I genuinely love flowers. It was a fun class where I could utilize my artistic abilities, and it would not be the typical rigorous academic college course. The woman teaching the course was European and the owner of a local floral shop. She was a vibrant professor with a very pleasant, caring nature. Her enthusiasm about floral arranging was evident. During our first class, she invited everyone to tour her store and showed us all of the floral designs and arrangements. It was a delightful experience.

During our first class, we were making simple arrangements when Larry bounded into the building shortly before the class ended. Our teacher noticed somebody walk into the building. She called to him, "Come in! We are just completing the projects."

Suddenly, I saw Larry's face redden. There were approximately eight students and all of them were girls. Larry felt incredibly uncomfortable, so he quietly seated himself on some stairs in the room, trying desperately to be as unobtrusive as possible. Because the teacher had singled him out so openly in class, he felt embarrassed and expressed later that he just felt like hiding. When I began packing up to leave, he breathed a sigh of relief.

"How'd it go tonight?" he asked as we left the building.

"Great!" I replied, showing him the arrangement I made.

"Wow! You did a good job with it!" he responded, admiring it. "Boy, did I ever feel stupid when I entered your class tonight. It didn't help to have your teacher so graciously invite me in. She practically announced my arrival to all your classmates."

"It's okay," I said encouragingly. "She wasn't trying to embarrass you. She just wanted to let you know that we were almost finished. None of us minded you watching us complete our projects. She is a really nice teacher. I don't think she'd intentionally make anyone feel uncomfortable."

I told Larry how much I'd enjoyed the class while we walked hand in hand back to the dormitory. On our way, I decided to offer Larry the arrangement I made. I thought he might enjoy it, and he gladly accepted it.

A few days later, Larry phoned me late one afternoon and asked, "Is there any way to preserve these flowers? They don't look as nice as they did a few days ago."

"Well, you can add preservatives to flowers to help them last longer, but sooner or later they're going to die. You just have to enjoy them while they last," I told him. "I wish there was some way to make them last, but I guess that's what we have to look forward to in heaven."

46

RACQUETBALL AND A
PHOTOGRAPH

That year, we received new student ID cards. When Larry saw my old card, he asked if I could keep it.

"Sure, go ahead," I responded. "I won't be needing it anymore. I should have a picture in my room as well. I'll find it and give it to you."

I found a picture that I had taken during high school and purchased a gold frame for it. Later that week, I presented it to Larry.

"When did you have this taken?" he asked. "You really had long hair then."

"Yeah, I did. That was my junior year in high school," I replied.

One evening a few days later, Larry told me that he had showed my picture to Noah, a quadriplegic student he worked with on campus.

"I told Noah a little about you. He liked your picture. Of course, I really admire it. I keep it on my dresser in my room."

Then Larry proceeded to tell me about how much he enjoyed his work for Noah. He always relished helping people. He was excellent at intuitively understanding how to help Noah. Because of Larry's remarkable skills, his work hours were extended. It was another indication that he had the capabilities of making an excellent physical therapist.

"Noah told me that he would like to have a girlfriend someday. He asked if I thought it could happen. It will be much harder for him," Larry said in a sad tone. "He has a lot more disadvantages to deal with than the majority of us do."

"Yeah, he does," I replied. "But God still could work things out." Then a verse from the Bible came to mind: "Nothing is impossible for God." Only God could provide for Noah's needs.

Larry matured immensely during the summer. He seemed more confident in himself. Also, he was much happier. Even acquaintances of Larry's noticed the difference in him. One day, I ran into a woman who had lived on my hall a few years before, and she told me how amazed she was by his change. "He told me that he loves life. He really seems so much happier this year! It is so nice to see that."

Yes, Larry did seem happier. Of course, I also knew that he was ecstatic to finally be officially dating me. I also knew that the summer was a wonderful experience for him. He genuinely enjoyed his time with Emilia's family and had really blossomed. One night in the cafeteria, Larry reminded me about what Emilia's mom said to him during the summer. She said, "You need girlfriend! When you get girlfriend?" He laughed thinking about it. "Now I can tell her that I have one," he said smiling. "She'll be happy."

Even though I saw a lot of positive changes in Larry, sometimes his insecurities would still get in the way. One day he said, "I know what you are doing for me, but what am I doing for you?"

"You are doing a lot!" I replied. "You're helping me to become more outgoing and to get out more so I don't stay in my room so much. And you're helping me become less afraid of racquetballs."

That quarter, I was taking a racquetball course to fulfill my physical education requirements. It was not one of my favorite sports. I was terribly frightened of the fast-flying racquetballs. One evening, Larry promised to go practice with me so that he could help me become a better racquetball player.

"I much prefer tennis," I disclosed to Larry that evening. "At least I'm not as paranoid of the balls. It's so much more difficult to play racquetball because I never know where the balls will go. They bounce all over the place."

"Yeah, they do, but there are some things to keep in mind. You can tell which direction the ball will head if you keep some basics in mind." Patiently, Larry worked with me to alleviate my worries and relieve my fear of the racquetball. With his assistance, I developed less fear about the sport and improved my techniques. I was thankful for his patience, his guidance, and his helpful advice. Although it would never be my favorite sport, or something I ever cared to play again, his sweet guidance helped me to conquer my fears. I would always be grateful for this.

47

THOMAS

One evening as we waited in line for cafeteria food, Larry began quietly singing a song to himself. I was surprised, because I recognized the lyrics: "Don't sit under an apple tree with anyone but me." Earlier during the summer, I'd taped some of my stepfather's music. He loved the music from the '30s and '40s. As a child, I frequently heard those songs, and I, too, immensely enjoyed the delightful, cheery tunes of that era.

"Where did you learn that song?" I asked with curiosity.

"My dad listens to songs like that. I learned it after listening to his music. I like that type of music, too."

"My dad listens to those songs, too," I said. "I love them as well. They are pleasant, cheery tunes, but I've never heard many people other than my dad or grandparents singing them. I just recorded a bunch of those silly tunes so I can listen to them."

I asked Larry if he knew some of the song titles I enjoyed. I was shocked that he knew them.

When we ate supper or lunch together, Larry introduced me to people I didn't know. One new person I met was a friend Larry had become familiar with during winter quarter when I was taking classes at a community college in my hometown. Thomas lived off campus with his grandparents but was originally from the West Coast. Larry and Thomas had become excellent friends. Both of them enjoyed physical activities and they participated in martial arts classes together.

Thomas wasn't as outgoing as Larry. There was a timid, bashful side to Thomas that Larry didn't have. Maybe the fact that Larry was much more outgoing than Thomas provided more balance to their relationship. Whatever the case, there was indeed a bond that drew them together as friends. Frequently, Thomas would attend vespers on Friday evenings with Larry and me. It was at one of the first vespers that autumn when Larry first introduced me to Thomas. Larry was always thrilled to have Thomas attend vespers with us.

One evening following my floral class, Larry and I took a leisurely stroll towards Lamson Hall. I had decorated a gorgeous basket with white frilly lace and elegant silk flowers.

"See what I made," I said showing Larry the arrangement. "I haven't seen Isabel for a long time. Why not surprise her and knock on her dorm window?"

Larry and I noisily knocked on her window and then concealed ourselves behind a bush. When she opened her window, we surprised her by popping out of the bushes.

"What are you guys doing sneaking around here? You both really surprised me! I wasn't sure who it was," Isabel told us. She had a gigantic smile on her face, and her dark eyes were sparkling. "Both of you seem so happy."

Isabel wasn't the first person to declare that we seemed happy. Heaps of people expressed that very same thought either verbally or nonverbally. Indeed, we were jovial. Our friends saw me in the cafeteria, at vespers, or at other activities more that quarter than they ever had. Everyone seemed to be pleased with the change.

Larry was constantly exploring the college newspaper for ideas on what activities to plan for the weekend. Each Friday, he'd present me with a list of activities that he'd clipped out of the paper, and we'd discuss what we wanted to do. Sometimes we considered one of the suggestions, but other times we were just satisfied with going to the beach. That was always one of the most popular weekend attractions for college students.

One Sabbath afternoon, Larry, Lauren, and I spent a pleasant afternoon walking along the beach and playing in the waves. It was one of those peaceful, calm, quiet Sabbath afternoons that you just wish could linger on forever. The sun was glistening, and the skies were filled with puffy white clouds. A gentle breeze provided the perfect weather for admiring the beach. It was wonderful. We couldn't have asked for a more perfect day, and it was a beautiful setting for our own worship service later that evening.

Those special days on the beaches near Andrews University will forever linger in my memory. I felt so thankful for the exquisite beauty of the view. It was breathtaking! As I listened to the waves lapping the shore and the chirping of sandpipers, I always felt so close to God. It was such a special place for all of us.

~48~

DREAMS

E ven now decades later, I keenly remember the moment in the silent, calm evening when I sat on the bridge with Larry, his arms enfolding me. It was then that I marveled at the beauty of life, the incredible miracle that God has given to each of us. God has control over our breath and over life. As I sat there, I thanked God for Larry's life and mine. I couldn't have been happier. The fragility of life entered my mind for a fleeting moment as I envisioned a couple who died because they succumbed to the chill of the winter night. Yes, things could happen to cause death, but I was appreciative God was in control. I was tremendously thankful for Larry's life.

Thank you, God, I contentedly prayed to myself.

At that moment, the thought of just how fragile life really is entered my mind for only a glimmering second and then quickly vanished from my thoughts. At the time, I could not fully grasp just how delicate it truly is. My mind quickly turned to happier thoughts as Larry and I lingered on the bridge, contentedly listening to the tranquil sounds of the autumn night.

"Where would you like to live?" Larry said, interrupting my thoughts.

"I'd like to live on the East Coast," I replied. Images sprung to my mind as I envisioned my dream home. "I've always wanted to live in the country where I can have a garden filled with flowers and a wonderful meadow. I'd love to live in an old stone cottage with a beautiful bay window overlooking the splendor of a floral garden."

"Have you ever thought about Colorado?"

"No," I responded. "I've never really had a desire to live on the West Coast. I know it's gorgeous and the weather is wonderful, but I've never wanted to live there."

"Have you ever been to Colorado?" he asked.

"No," I answered.

"It's gorgeous." I could see the sparkle in Larry's eyes as he described the beauty that he'd observed while on vacation there. "There's lots of country there, too. The mountains are what I enjoy the most. I'm sure there are lots of places where you could grow flowers there, too."

"I guess I'd never really thought about Colorado," I said. *With love, though, I guess there are always compromises,* I thought to myself. Two people can never share the exact same visions, but together they can enhance them and labor to resolve the differences. I guess I could agree on a different location to live as long as I'd be with Larry.

"I'd love to have horses, too," I said. "When I was about seven, my cousin had a horse, and we had a pony. My brother and I frequently went horseback riding with my cousin. We'd go riding through the vineyards near our home. I really enjoyed it! It sure would be wonderful to do that again."

"Horses are nice," Larry responded. "I love the horse I have at home. I've always enjoyed riding it."

We sat there for a long time, listening to the pleasant evening sounds. It was so peaceful and still. I enjoyed the quietness.

"Are you getting cold?" Larry asked after a while. It was one of those windy autumn evenings in which the temperature steadily drops. Although we had brought a blanket with us, the nip in the air could still be felt.

"Well, I'm a little cold, but I'm not ready to leave yet."

Larry wrapped the blanket more securely around my shoulders.

"I wish we didn't have to go to school. It would be so nice to be free from its burdens. I wish we had time to do this every evening. I love you so much. I wish I could be with you always," I said as I gave him a hug.

"Won't it be nice when we get to heaven? We won't have to worry about anything then. We can always be together," Larry said.

We lingered on the thought of how spectacular a place heaven will be. It would be a glorious place, free from suffering and pain. We sat in deep reflection on that quiet evening. The coolness of the air was chilling me, and I realized that we would have to leave soon. I could just picture a headline in the paper stating that two college students had been found dead on a bridge after succumbing to the cold weather.

"I guess we should get going," I said gloomily. "I'm beginning to really get cold and sitting isn't helping much."

"Okay," Larry agreed. "Let's go."

Larry picked me up in his arms, determined to carry me up Pathfinder Hill. At the foot of the hill, I prompted him to put me down. It was quite a steep hill, and I felt that it was enough work for one person to ascend. Grudgingly, Larry put me down, and hand in hand we leisurely ascended the hill that resounded from memories of the happy moments Larry and I shared together. Slowly, we strolled along towards the girls' dorm. Before we arrived at the doors of the dorm, Larry and I said goodnight.

I was surprised to discover Lauren in my room when I entered. She was chatting with Sophie. I hadn't seen much of either of them that week, and so we stayed up talking. My plans had been to prepare for bed earlier that night, but as usual my noble intentions were shattered. Of course, both Sophie and Lauren were anxious to hear about the events of my evening, and I was bubbling over with enthusiasm. Larry was always bursting full of surprises, and I could hardly wait to share the events from that evening with my friends.

"You wouldn't believe what Larry did tonight," I began. "Before we headed to the bonfire tonight at my friend's house, Larry insisted that we stop by the grocery store to buy some crackers to take over with us. I waited in the car for him. A few minutes later, he returned with a gigantic smile on his face and handed me a bouquet of roses. I couldn't believe it! He really surprised me with them. Aren't they pretty?" I said as I unwrapped the flowers and filled a vase with water.

For some reason that night, our discussion turned to things that we'd unearthed during our devotions that week. We enthusiastically discussed texts from the Bible. Lauren shared several wonderful texts from Isaiah, and I read promises that helped me survive another hectic week. It was almost 11:30 by the time we joined hands and prayed. Each of us prayed, taking turns thanking God for the blessings that He bestowed on us that week and praying for each other and for all of our friends. The feeling of camaraderie and fellowship was almost overpowering and meant the world to me then. It will be forever etched into my heart and mind.

THE ST. JOSEPH PIER

I went to bed that Friday evening smiling and joyful, unaware of the enormous danger that Larry and Thomas were facing at that moment. My mind passed into a peaceful slumber and I arose early the next morning to prepare for work. As I sat at the desk that morning, I read passages from the book of Isaiah. Before I knew it, 6:30 had arrived. Sitting at the reception desk, I noticed Sophie approaching me in the hallway. It was wonderful to see her, but her expression made me wonder if something was wrong.

"My cousin called this morning and mentioned something about Larry and then asked if you were around," Sophie said. "I told him you were sleeping and then realized you were at work, but we'd hung up by then so I couldn't tell him. I thought you'd like to know. It sounds like Larry might be in trouble. Do you know where Larry went last night when you came back to the dorm?"

"Well," I said, pausing to remember. "He told me he might go to the beach with Thomas. I was concerned about it, since it was cold and windy last night. I hinted that I didn't think it was a good idea, but he didn't mention it any further after that."

Anxiety, trepidation, and alarm filled my thoughts. Was something wrong? Had something terrible happened to Larry? He hadn't phoned me that morning like he normally did, but I forced that thought out of my mind. He was probably just sleeping.

"Maybe your cousin called because Larry got back after curfew last night," I said. The possibility that Larry may have returned late that night eased my mind, but as the next few hours progressed, a note of panic and concern arose in my mind and heart. Something was desperately wrong, but I shoved the horrific thought from my mind as sleepiness overcame me.

Finally, 8:30 arrived. It was a welcome sight to spot Lauren relieving me from work.

"It's so good to see you," I told her. "I'm practically falling asleep."

Lauren and I chatted for a few minutes. "Larry hasn't phoned this morning. Sophie told me the deans from the men's dorm called early this morning wondering if Sophie knew where Larry was. He probably just got to bed late and is still asleep," I said in an effort to appease my own concern. Lauren and I both knew, though, that it wasn't normal for Larry not to phone.

"I'll pray for you," Lauren replied as I turned to leave.

"Thanks," I nervously responded. I was desperately going to need her prayers. I started back towards my dorm. As I neared my room, I bumped into Dean Fredrick in the hallway. She was talking to my suitemate, Lindsey. My heart sank when I saw her. I knew that something was wrong.

Dean Fredrick gently grabbed me by the arm when she noticed me. "I need to talk to you," I heard her saying. "Let's go down to the chaplain's office."

My heart sank and a large knot caught in my throat. I prayed silently and we descended the steps to the main floor of Lamson Hall.

Before I knew it, we were both seated in the small office.

"This is hard for me to say," she slowly began. "Last night, Larry went to the pier at St. Joseph with Thomas. A wave caught him, Debbie," she said with huge tears in her eyes. She paused for a few moments and then continued. "They never found his body."

She put her arms around me as sobs shook my body. All I could think was that Larry was gone forever, and the words that I had been aching to tell him that morning could never be said.

Looking back on that dismal Sabbath morning, I still remember the immeasurable sorrow I felt. It's incredible to think that a morning that had begun so peacefully could end in such deep-seated sadness. Thankfully, though, God provided for my needs that bleak autumn day. I was fortunate to be surrounded by people who cared: friends, deans, pastors, family members, and even people I hardly even knew. Everyone who heard about the tragedy that day paused to pray for the family and friends of Larry. I was so thankful to be surrounded by such Christian individuals. I was desperately going to need their support in the agonizing days to come. That morning, the campus pastor offered some wonderful words of assurance to all gathered in the room with me. He shared a passage entitled "God's Plans the Best" from the book *Ministry of Healing*. The words that ministered to my heart from that excerpt were:

In the future life the mysteries that here have annoyed and disappointed us will be made plain. We shall see that our seemingly unanswered prayers and disappointed hopes have been among our greatest blessings.[5]

Not all of the words that the pastor expressed that day penetrated my grief-stricken mind, but at least I grasped the major points that were being said. His words would provide tremendous comfort to me:

Often your mind may be clouded because of pain. Then do not try to think. You know that Jesus loves you. He understands your weakness. You may do His will by simply resting in His arms.[6]

Those were words that would especially bring comfort in the days to follow. God understood my sorrow, and indeed His arms of love were enveloping me. He would always continue to be there for me and for everyone else who grieved Larry's loss. I embraced God as hot tears streamed from my eyes. I desperately needed His strength and His courage to tell Larry goodbye for the last time.

"*Debbie,*" I could hear the Lord saying, "*remember that Larry is resting right now, free from the pain and hardships of this earth. Someday soon, Debbie, I will return, and I will raise Larry from the dead, and you will be reunited with him again. What a wonderful day that will be! I know that you are hurting now, Debbie, but take my hand. I will comfort you and embrace you when you need it so that you can cry on my shoulder. I know it hurts, but I only expect you to take it one day at a time. I will lead you step-by-step. I will bring the comfort that you need."*

I could feel the embrace of God comforting me and felt His hands wiping the tears from my eyes. Indeed, He would help me.

"Goodbye, Larry. I will see you in the morning when the Lord raises you from your peaceful slumber. I cannot wait until that glorious day when Jesus returns again. I will always miss you. What a wonderful reunion that will be. Good night. Call me in the morning. I will be waiting and looking forward to it. Adiós. ¡Te amo! Goodbye, Larry. I love you! See you in the morning."

CONCLUSION

I am extremely thankful for the friends and individuals who drew near to encourage me during the difficult time following Larry's death. Their thoughtful words, cards, and letters were a great encouragement and support to me. I would especially like to share the reassuring words my friend Lauren wrote to me. Her words would provide tremendous comfort in the upcoming days. It is my prayer that all of you may gain courage and strength from her words. She has provided some wonderful texts from the Bible. I urge each of you to find these texts in your own Bibles and to search for other texts of inspiration. There are so many wonderful gems spread throughout the Bible that can provide strength. I implore each of you to hunt for them. Indeed, you will discover a powerful source of strength, hope, and encouragement in the scriptures. May God provide each of you with comfort, peace, and hope! Lean into His arms and know He is continually there to love and help you.

My Dearest Deb (and all of Larry's friends and family),

We are both going to acutely miss and do miss Larry's presence, his willingness to help and please those around him, his enthusiasm for life, and his sunny disposition. We've experienced a terrible, unexplainable, and indescribable loss... Our hearts are heavy with grief, deeply aching and longing fiercely to be with our precious Larry. Nothing or no one can take his place, and the emptiness and hollowness that has been left instead will never be refilled until at last when we go home to meet our Redeemer, our Savior, our Creator and Friend. Oh, what a glorious day that will be to see our Lord face-to-face and to finally and forever be with our loved ones who now rest in Jesus!!! All our intense sorrow and sense of loss, our indescribable pain and unrelenting grief that we experience so acutely now, will then be replaced with joy and everlasting comfort, knowing that never, never again, will we ever be separated from anyone by the terribly excruciating pangs and anguish of death. Death will no longer have power over us because we will be redeemed and taken to be forever with our Lord and Savior, and to be with those whom we love so intensely. In this we have hope and find comfort for this trying and most difficult hour. It is our privilege, both now and forever, to rest in the precious arms of Jesus, that both strengthen and sustain us, knowing that He will care for us and see *us through this dark, confusing, and seemingly unending suffocating maze. He will take us by the hand and lead us step-by-step, both encouraging and reassuring us forward through His tremendous love and understanding. It is because He <u>does</u> understand and experiences our grief that He <u>can</u> and <u>will</u> comfort us and help us cope in the awful and devastating hour. He loves us, Deb. Never forget that. He doesn't welcome death any more than we do. He, the Creator and Sustainer of life, never intended for us to experience the terrible grips and claws of death and right now He aches right along with us. Deb, we live in a sin-stricken world, but even so, it's our privilege to lean on Jesus, look to our Savior, know He will always be there for us, to wipe away our tears and eventually heal our grief. And one great, glorious, joyful day, reunite us with those we love and now miss so much. Just as He shares our sorrow, Jesus will also one day share our joy. It will be His utmost pleasure and indescribable joy to bring us together again with our precious Larry, so dear to our hearts, and with all our other loved ones.*

I would like to share some Bible texts with you, Deb, that have been a great source of comfort to me. I pray that they are a blessing to you both now and in the days, months, and years to come.

II Thessalonians 2:16, 17

"May our Lord Jesus Christ Himself, and God, and Father, who has loved us, and given us everlasting consolation and good hope by grace, comfort your hearts, and establish you in every good word and work..."

Psalm 34:15, 17-19, 22

"The eyes of the Lord are on the righteous, and His ears are open to their cry... The righteous cry out, and the Lord hears, and delivers them out of all their troubles. The Lord is near to those who have a broken heart; and saves such as have a contrite spirit. Many are the afflictions of the righteous: but the Lord delivers him out of them all... The Lord redeems the soul of His servants: and none of those who trust in Him shall be desolate."

Psalm 116:1-6

"I love the Lord, because He has heard my voice and my supplications. Because He has inclined His ear to me, therefore I will call upon Him as long as I live. The sorrows of death encompassed me... I found trouble and sorrow. Then I called upon the name of the Lord; O Lord, I implore you, deliver my soul. Gracious is the Lord, and righteous; yes our God is merciful. The

Lord preserves the simple: I was brought low and He helped me."

Psalm 145:14
"The Lord upholds all that fall, and raises up all those that are bowed down."

I Timothy 1:1
"God our Savior, and Lord Jesus Christ is our hope."

Hebrews 13:5
"I will never leave thee, nor forsake thee."

James 4:8
"Draw near to God and He will draw near to you."

Psalm 4:5
"Put your trust in the Lord."

II Corinthians 4:8, 9, 18
"We are troubled on every side, yet not distressed; we are perplexed, but not in despair, persecuted, but not forsaken; cast down, but not destroyed. While we look not to the things which are seen: for the things which are seen are temporal; but the things which are not seen are eternal."

God has not promised that the Christian walk will be easy, but He has promised that He will help us through the obstacles and trials that stand in our way.

II Kings 20:5

"I have heard your prayer, I have seen your tears: behold I will heal you."

I Peter 5:7, 10

"Cast all your care upon Him for He cares for you… But the God of all grace, who called us to His eternal glory by Christ Jesus, after you have suffered a while, make you perfect, establish, strengthen and settle you." (NKJV)

"Cast all your anxiety on Him because He cares for you. The God of all grace, who called you to His eternal glory in Christ, after you have suffered a little while, will Himself restore you and make you strong, firm and steadfast." (NIV)

Matthew 5:4

"Blessed are those who mourn for they shall be comforted."

Psalm 147:3

"He heals the brokenhearted and binds up their wounds."

Isaiah 30:18-21

"Therefore the Lord will wait, that He may be gracious to you; and therefore will He be exalted, that He may have mercy on you: for the Lord is a God of justice: blessed are all those who wait for Him. For... you shall weep no more. He will be very gracious to you at the sound of your cry; when He hears it, He will answer you. And though the Lord gives you the bread of adversity and the water of affliction, yet your teachers will not be moved into a corner anymore, but your eyes shall see your teachers: And your ears shall hear a word behind you, saying, this is the way, walk in it, whenever you turn to the right hand, or whenever you turn to the left."

John 14:6

"I am the Way, the Truth, and the Life.

Isaiah 43:1, 2

"Thus says the Lord who created you...and He who formed you...Fear not: for I have redeemed you, I have called you by your name; you are mine. When you pass through the waters, I will be with you; and through the rivers, they shall not overflow you: when you walk through the fire, you will not be burned; nor shall the flame scorch you."

Isaiah 61:1-3

"The Spirit of the Lord God is upon me; because the Lord hath anointed me to preach good tidings unto the meek; he hath sent me to bind up the brokenhearted, to proclaim liberty to the captives, and the opening of the prison to them that are bound; to proclaim the acceptable year of the Lord...to comfort all that mourn; to appoint unto them beauty for ashes, the oil of joy for mourning, the garment of praise for the spirit of heaviness; that they might be called the trees of righteousness, the planting of the Lord, that He might be glorified."

No matter what happens, God is ever a source of strength and comfort. He can console our deepest hurts and heal our deepest wounds and most intense grief.

Hebrews 4:15, 16

"For we have not a High Priest who is unable to sympathize with our weaknesses, but we have One who has been tempted in every way, just as we are— yet without sin. Let us then approach the throne of grace with confidence, so that we may receive mercy and find grace to help us in our time of need." (NIV)

I Corinthians 10:13

"No suffering or pain that comes your way is beyond

the course of what others have had to face. All you need to remember is that God is compassionate and trustworthy. He will never let you be pushed past your limit. He will provide a way out so you can stand up under it."

Isaiah 41:9, 10, 13

"You are my servant; I have chosen you; I have chosen you and have not rejected you. So do not fear, for I am with you, do not be dismayed, for I am you God. I will strengthen you; I will uphold you with my righteous right hand. For I am the Lord, your God, who takes hold of your right hand and says to you. Do not fear; I will help you."

Jeremiah 29:11-14

"'For I know the plans I have for you,' declares the Lord 'plans to prosper you and not to harm you, plans to give you hope and a future. Then you will call upon me and come and pray to me, and I will listen to you. You will seek me and find me when you seek me with all your heart. I will be found of you,' declares the Lord."

Jeremiah 31:3, 4, 9, 13, 14, 17, 25, 26

"I have loved you with an everlasting love; I have drawn you with loving-kindness, I will build you

up again and you will be rebuilt. They will come with weeping; they will pray as I lead them. I will turn their mourning into gladness. I will give them comfort and joy instead of sorrow. I will satisfy the soul... My people shall be satisfied with my goodness says the Lord. There is hope for your future declares the Lord. For I have satisfied the weary soul, and I have replenished every sorrowful soul." (NIV and NKJV)

Jeremiah 33:3, 6

"Call upon me, and I will answer you, and show you great and mighty things, you do not know. I will bring health and healing to it; I will heal my people and will let them enjoy abundant peace and security." (NIV).

Lamentations 3:22-26, 32, 33, 55-58

"Because of the Lord's great love we are not consumed, for His compassions never fail. They are new every morning; great is your faithfulness. I will say to myself, 'The Lord is my portion; therefore will I wait for Him.' The Lord is good to those whose hope is in Him, to the one who seeks Him; it is good to wait quietly for the salvation of the Lord. Though He brings grief, He will show compassion, so great is His unfailing love. For He does not willingly bring affliction or grief to the children of men. I called on your name, O Lord, from

the depths of the pit. You heard my plea: 'Do not close your ears to my cry for relief.' You came near when I called you, and You said, 'Do not fear.'"

Psalm 24:14

"Wait on the Lord; be of good courage, and He shall strengthen your heart; wait I say on the Lord."

Psalm 31:24

"Be of good courage, and He shall strengthen your heart, all ye that hope in the Lord."

Psalm 29:11

"The Lord will give strength to His people; the Lord will bless His people with peace."

Joshua 1:5, 9

"As I was with Moses, so I will be with you. I will not leave you, nor forsake you. Be strong and of good courage, be not afraid, neither be dismayed: for the Lord your God is with you wherever you go."

I Corinthians 15:51-58

"In a moment, in the twinkling of an eye, at the last trump: for the trumpet shall sound, and the dead shall be raised incorruptible, and we shall be changed. For this corruptible must put on incorruption, and this mortal must put on immortality. So when this *corruptible shall have put on incorruption, and this mortal shall have put on immortality, then shall be brought to pass the saying that is written, death is swallowed up in victory. O death, where is thy sting? O grave where is thy victory? The sting of death is sin; and the strength of sin is the law. But thanks be to God, which giveth us the victory through our Lord Jesus Christ. Therefore, my beloved brethren, be ye steadfast, immovable, always abounding in the work of the Lord, forasmuch as ye know that your labor is not in vain in the Lord."*

I Thessalonians 4:14-18

"For if we believe that Jesus died and rose again, even so then also which sleep in Jesus will God bring with Him. For this we say unto you by the word of the Lord, that we which are alive and remain unto the coming of the Lord shall not prevent them which are asleep. For the Lord Himself shall descend from Heaven with a shout, with the voice of the archangel, and with the trump of God: and the dead in Christ shall rise first: then we which are alive and remain shall be caught up together with Him in the clouds, to meet the Lord in the air: and so shall we ever be with the Lord. Wherefore, comfort one another with these words."

Isaiah 25:8, 9

"He will swallow up death in victory; and the Lord God will wipe away all tears from off of all faces; and the rebuke of His people shall He take away from off all the earth: for the Lord has spoken it. And it shall be said in that day, Lo this is our God; we have waited for Him, and He will save us; this is the Lord; we have waited for Him, we will be glad and rejoice in His salvation."

Revelation 21:4, 5

"And God shall wipe away all tears from their eyes; and there shall be no more death, neither sorrow, nor crying, neither shall there be any more pain: for the former things are passed away. Behold I make all things new."

Isaiah 51:11, 12

"Therefore the redeemed of the Lord shall return, and come with singing unto Zion; and everlasting joy shall be upon their heads: they shall obtain gladness and joy; and sorrow and mourning shall flee away. I, even I am He who comforts you."

Isaiah 26:3, 4, 12

"You will keep him in perfect peace, whose mind is stayed on You: because he trusts in you. Trust in the

Lord forever: for in the Lord Jehovah is everlasting strength. Lord, you will ordain peace for us: for you also have done all our works in us."

Psalm 23

"The Lord is my Shepherd; I shall not want. He makes me to lie down in green pastures: He leads me beside the still waters. He restores my soul: He leads me in the paths of righteousness for His name's sake. Yea, though I walk through the valley of the shadow of death, I will fear no evil: for You are with me. Your rod and Your staff comfort me. You prepare a table before me in the presence of my enemies: You anoint my head with oil; my cup runs over. Surely goodness and mercy shall follow me all the days of my life: and I will dwell in the house of the Lord forever."

II Corinthians 1:3–5

"Blessed be God, even the Father of our Lord Jesus Christ, the Father of mercies, and the God of all comfort; who comforts us in all our tribulation, that we may be able to comfort those who are in any trouble, with the comfort with which we ourselves are comforted by God. For as the sufferings of Christ abound in us, so our consolation also abounds through Christ."

II Corinthians 4:8, 9, 16, 17-18

We are hard pressed on every side, but not crushed; perplexed, but not in despair; persecuted, but not abandoned; struck down, but not destroyed. Therefore, we do not lose heart... For our light and momentary troubles are achieving for us an eternal glory that far outweighs them all. So we must fix our eyes not on what is seen, but on what is unseen. For what is seen is temporary, but what is unseen is eternal."

Romans 8:28

"And we know that all things work together for good to those who love God, to those who are called according to His purpose."

Romans 15:13

"Now may the God of hope fill you with all joy and peace in believing that ye may abound in hope, through the power of the Holy Ghost."

II Corinthians 13:14

"The grace of the Lord Jesus Christ, and the Love of God, and the communion of the Holy Ghost, be with you. Amen."

Deb, there are many more texts in the Bible that will be of comfort to you, but I hope these have been helpful. As you continue to pray and study your Bible, may the Lord guide you to many more beautiful texts. I love you, Debbie, and am praying for you. Don't give up your faith, but remain steadfast in Jesus's love."

With all my love,

Lauren

EPILOGUE

I was twenty-two years old, one month shy of twenty-three, when Larry drowned. We had been formally dating for three weeks, but we'd been tremendous friends who had been informally going out with each other for two years. It was simple, but we did many things together in those two years. There was continually a request for some new adventure, and in the simple pleasures of life we enjoyed ourselves. Those wonderful times had suddenly vanished. Grief consumed me.

All around, life continued, but my life was at a complete standstill. It was supposed to be a blissful, ecstatic, joyful time as I was almost finished with my undergraduate degree. I should have been celebrating, but instead I was just barely surviving. Melancholy hung thickly around me, consuming me until I could hardly move.

My heart ached for Larry; my entire body throbbed. Being on campus with the numerous memories just about destroyed me. It hurt so much to turn the corners of campus and remember the joy and enthusiasm I had once felt. Even the memories of Larry waving and shouting to me from across campus plagued me with pain. Moving on was exceptionally difficult. How can one move on after such a tragedy? Is it even possible?

I wondered if I'd ever make it. All I ached for was to throw in the towel and walk away. But I had to continue trudging on. Somehow, I had to force myself through my pain and complete the final weeks of that quarter so I could obtain my degree. I went to each of my professors and requested that they give me one week off of classes so I could recover. They promised to help in any way they could.

The week following Larry's death was a busy one, because my friends and I had to prepare for Larry's memorial service. We wrote his eulogy, and somehow, I had to find a way to collect myself enough to attend that service.

I'm not sure what all happened in the weeks following Larry's death. All I know is that frequently in the evenings I would slip out of my room and wander through campus alone, sobbing, aching, desperate for my pain to dissipate. I hurt so deeply that sometimes it made me sick. As I walked, I prayed and cried.

One evening as tears streamed from my eyes, I backed into an evergreen tree, begging for God to somehow help me. As I stood there, I could feel the arms of the tree embracing me. It was as if God was reaching out His arms to surround me with His love. Peace flowed through me during that moment. God was there with me journeying through my pain.

I traveled through that quarter one step at a time, with God at my side. When the quarter concluded, my professors gladly agreed to write the required letters so I could apply to a graduate program. Thanks to them, I was accepted into graduate school the following year.

When my final quarter was finished at Andrews University, I had to leave immediately. Memories were everywhere, and it hurt so much to remember that I simply had to flee. God opened the doors for a task force position at a boarding academy, which would keep my mind busy during the daytime hours and allow me to write at the night when I was unable to sleep. During that time of sleepless nights and endless tears, I began writing the book that would eventually bring healing to my broken, wounded heart. I wrote hour after hour, reliving the special memories I had with Larry. I was eager to share the incredible person he was. Writing was the outlet for my pain.

As I look back over the years, the pain of Larry's death is still vivid. I still miss him and long to see him again. The pain is still real. I still cry. The physical items he gave me became too painful to retain. To move on required that I relinquish the items that caused me to hurt so deeply. What I learned to do was to hold onto the memories. I learned to keep those special times we shared deep inside my heart and mind. They are the memories I captured in this book. Indeed, it is these joyful memories that keep me going. They are the memories I'll hold on to forever. His motto is also what keeps me going. The memory of his life will forever linger in my heart.

Twenty-five years have passed since the painful events of Larry's death. I completed my master's degree in speech pathology three years after he died. Since that time, I have been working as a pediatric speech therapist, trying my best to provide hope, help, and encouragement to the families and children I work with.

I'd love to say that I found another prince charming whom I married and had a family with, but the man I later married was not a prince charming. He was abusive. He happened to be the same person that my friend told me was a better fit than Larry. She was wrong. I had to divorce him and somehow collect the pieces of my life and raise my two children as a single parent. But that story is for another book.

Whether or not there is anyone else for me on this earth now, I have the most amazing memory of someone who was dear to me. I will always keep his memory, and his life will always remain close to my heart. Larry was a very special person, and I am so thankful he was in my life.

Now, decades later, I hope that my life will capture the theme that Larry's life held. May I be an encouragement and help to all who surround me in my work and in my community, to my friends and my family. I hope and pray that others will see hope through the life I've lived.

Life is filled with pain and anguish, but God promises to help each of us through those painful times. My prayer is that all of you will learn to hold on to God despite the incredible challenges and heartaches that you face. Life is never easy, but God promises to journey through life with us if we will allow him to. As we face trials and tribulations, may we always remember that God is an ever-present source of strength. He will continue to help us. May we never, ever forget that.

EULOGY

L arry was a dear friend who will be greatly missed. He was exceptionally caring and thoughtful and really went out of his way to help others. Nothing gave him greater pleasure than sharing his time and talents with those around him. He often did not realize he went the second or third mile. Larry always put others first. He anticipated their needs and kept a step ahead, thinking of ways to fulfill those needs. He was very optimistic and enthusiastic about life, always seeing the brighter side of things. His smile cheered those with whom he came in contact. His attempts to brighten others' lives did not bring attention to himself and were not always noticed by those around him. It was often his simple acts, which came so genuinely and naturally, that made Larry the special person he was. Larry's little acts of love, woven into others' lives, day by day, truly reflect God's love for us. Larry truly showed his friends and family the importance of other people and their value to God. The following poem portrays the motive that governed Larry's life.

When morning breaks and I face the day
This dear Lord, is what I pray.
That when the same day fades to gray,
Some child of yours may happier be,
May find himself more close to Thee,
Because I lived this day.

Jule Creaser[7]

Now Only Stories Can Be Told

My mind travels down many roads of thought:
Times of laughter and happiness
Others of sadness and grief.
As I remember stories and happenings of days gone by
I wonder why sometimes they bring pain.

Only happy thoughts fill my mind now,
But suddenly I pause; the happiness ends.
I am left with tears of sorrow and grief
Because now only stories can be told.
Now, only stories can be told.

I sit as hot tears stream from my eyes.
Many things now cause pain:
Pictures, waves on the coast, roses, gifts…
"Why," God I ask, "did my joy so suddenly end?"
Can't you see my sorrow or feel my pain?"

Briefly I see his image and hear him calling my name.
"God, please take me away from this world of pain.
I long for my friend! Can't I see him again?"
Because now only stories can be told.
Now, only stories can be told.

Debbie Gordon

The Plan of the Master Weaver

Our lives are but fine weavings
That God and we prepare
Each life becomes a fabric planned
And fashioned in His care
We may not always see just how the weavings intertwine
But we must trust the Master's hand
And follow His design
For He can view the pattern
Upon the upper side
While we must look from underneath
And trust in Him to guide
Sometimes a strand of sorrow
Is added to His plan
And though it's difficult for us
We still must understand
That it's He who fills the shuttle
It's He who knows what's best
So we must weave in patience
And leave to Him the rest
Not till the loom is silent
And the shuttles cease to fly
Shall God unroll the canvas
And explain the reason why
The darker threads are as needed

In the weaver's skillful hand
As the threads of gold and silver
In the pattern He has planned.

Author Unknown [8]

Just When I Need Him Most

Just when I need Him, Jesus is near,
Just when I falter, just when I fear;
Ready to help me, ready to cheer,

Just when I need Him most
Just when I need Him most,
Just when I need Him most,
Jesus is near to comfort and cheer,
Just when I need Him most.

Just when I need Him, Jesus is true,
Never forsaking, all the way through;
Giving for burdens pleasures anew,
Jesus is near to comfort and cheer,

Just when I need Him most.
Just when I need Him most
Just when I need Him most,
Jesus is near to comfort and cheer,
Just when I need Him most.

Just when I need Him, Jesus is strong,
Bearing my burdens all the day long;
For all my sorrow giving a song,
Just when I need Him most.

Just when I need Him most
Just when I need Him most,
Just when I need Him most,
Jesus is near to comfort and cheer,
Just when I need Him most.

Just when I need Him, He is my all,
Answering when upon Him I call;
Tenderly watching lest I should fall,
Just when I need Him most.

Just when I need Him most
Just when I need Him most,
Just when I need Him most,
Jesus is near to comfort and cheer,
Just when I need Him most.

William C. Poole [9]

Side by Side[3]

Side by side we stand
Awaiting God's command
Worshiping the saving king
Living by His grace
And moving on in faith
Jesus himself will see us thru'

Meet me in heaven
We'll join hands together
Meet me by the savior's side
I'll meet you in heaven
We'll sing songs together
Brothers and sisters, I'll be there

Soldiers all are we
To go where Jesus leads
We'll fight the foe
And we will overcome
Heaven is our goal
To save every soul
Pray that we all will be there.

Meet me in heaven
We'll join hands together

Eulogy

Meet me by the savior's side
I'll meet you in heaven
We'll sing songs together
Brothers and sisters, I'll be there
(Praise the lord we all will be there)

LETTER TO LARRY

October 14, 2017

Dear Larry,

I woke up this morning with the desire to talk to you. Almost twenty-five years have passed since the night you went to the pier with Thomas. Often, I have ached for the events of that night to be different, for you to have listened to my plea to not go to the pier that stormy night. Many spoke about how you received a phone call that night from a friend who was upset and that caused you to want to go to the pier that night. Others talked about the pain that was inside you. Your dad talked about the trials you faced as a child and with your peers. Others have asked if it was an attempt to die by suicide. Whatever happened and whatever was going through your mind that night, none of us know; only God does. My mind has always focused on the fact that, when we are young, we take risks and don't realize how dangerous things can be. We seem invincible. Death is not something most young adults think about. I remember you talking about your plan to go with Thomas that night. Thomas talked about how you ran out to the unsafe part of the pier despite his cries for you to come back. He knew it wasn't safe. Many questions raced through people's minds as they tried desperately to make sense of what happened. My heart has forever hurt for Thomas because he felt so guilty for taking you there that night. I told him that it wasn't his fault that you drowned. You made the choice to run beyond the fenced areas of the pier. But the pain of those events still hurt Thomas. They hurt all of us.

For some odd reason, my mind didn't stay on the questions. It has been consumed with pain, grief, sorrow, and anguish. It felt like I was in a tunnel that was so black I couldn't find my way. There was no light, and the painful memories on campus about crushed me. Everywhere I turned, I could see your image, and I was reminded of all the things we did together. At night, I would wander through campus and cry. Sleepless nights consumed me. I would cry so hard that it would make me sick. My entire body hurt, and my mind was clouded with pain. It was difficult to make it through the remaining weeks of fall quarter.

For twenty-five years, all I have ached for is to talk to you. Sometimes the desire to hear your voice on the phone consumes me. I ache to have another conversation with you and to hear your analogies. The memories of that special time remain in my heart and mind. They are what keep me going, but there are times they paralyze me with pain, too. Even now, all I want is to have you back. But my wish will never come true here on this earth. I must wait for heaven.

I want you to know that I am grateful for the time we had together. Often, I have thanked God for the patience you had for me. Insecurities, shyness, pain, and all, you accepted me and continued to pursue me. Thank you for never giving up on me and for your patience and understanding. I needed that so much at that time. Over the years, I have wished more people were like you. But I am thankful for you, as you were the person I needed all those years ago. It helped me find my way. I'm also thankful you taught me the importance of being kind to others and helping people in need. This has been something I have tried to instill in my children's lives, and it has been important to me as well. After your death, I wanted my life to make a difference in others' lives, because I realized how short life really is. Thank you so much for teaching me this.

I wish you could have received your degree as a physical therapist, because I know you would have been such a blessing to so many people. Watching how patient, kind, and thoughtful you were told me it was the right field for you. Often, I have longed to work with you in the field of rehabilitation, but that desire cannot be filled.

Why am I so torn to shreds even now with your death? Tears, grief, and heartache have been washing over me recently, making my days difficult to handle. I feel the same feelings I struggled with so long ago. Not a day goes by that I don't miss you. The desire for you will never leave me, but I can't change anything. We have been separated forever on this earth, so I will always have days when the pain of your loss consumes me. This is part of grief, and I hate it. You were taken from me too soon.

The memories of the person you were still flood my mind. Few people have your heart. You cared. Daily, you tried to make everyone's life better, and I so appreciated that. You were so much fun to be around and came up with creative things to do. Your enthusiasm was contagious. We all appreciated you. I hope and pray I captured the person I remember you being in my book. I loved and appreciated you so much. If only things had ended differently. But, again, I am thankful I met you, for the two years we had together, and for all you taught me.

I ache to go sledding down Pathfinder Hill again on those cafeteria trays, go on long walks with you, go to the beach and church with you, or go on another adventure you come up with. It would be awesome to relive those amazing days. Thank you for giving me such wonderful memories to live on. They are what keep me going. Your memory and life will always remain deeply in my heart. Thank you, Larry, for loving me, weaknesses and all. Thank you for all our amazing phone calls. I will never forget you. I cannot wait to see you again. Until then, you will continue to live in my heart. I love you.

Love,
Debbie

SOULMATES

Larry and I were soulmates. It isn't often that we find a soulmate in this life. When we do, they teach us so many things. He blessed my life so much. I made it through my undergraduate degree because of him. But his life taught me so much, too.

I have always been uncomfortable around men, but Larry was the exception. I always felt comfortable with him. As an introvert, I learned that I do best in small groups. This helps ease my shyness and social anxiety. His gentle, pleasant spirit calmed me and put me at ease. He was like a comfortable pair of old jeans. I knew I could talk to him about anything. We connected deeply, like we had always known each other. It felt so normal to be with him. We just fit together in a way I never could have imagined. His life taught me more about myself.

Nature is something we both enjoyed. We didn't need fancy pleasures; all we needed was time together enjoying the simple activities of life. He taught me how to have fun with the simple things. His life also taught me the importance of caring for others. But, more than anything, he taught me that a relationship starts with a friendship. And friendship and conversation, not physical touch, should be the foundation of a relationship. Our friendship was a special one, a once-in-a-lifetime one. I am continually reminded of the blessing he was to me.

He may be gone, but his spirit and legacy continue to live inside of me. The memories of that long-ago time are what keep me going. I pray that I shared it with the depth, love, care, enthusiasm, and spark that Larry had. He definitely was a special person.

I hope that his story, his legacy, will touch each and every one of you that read these words. May each of you grow because of the person who lived in the stories I shared. My hope is that his life will be remembered and that it will light a spark in each person who comes to know him through this book. Life needs more people who care, inspire, encourage, and provide hope. Our world needs more Larry Borgs in it. May his legacy light our world today.

AFTERWORD

I still keep in touch with my college friends. We recall our years at Andrews with fond memories. All of my friends have gone on to be amazing people. Paul is a gifted counselor and public speaker who owns his own private practice. Sophie became an accountant and married Rob, and they have two boys. Lauren became a teacher and married Jeff, and they have four children. Thomas eventually married. Camille married and had one child, and she works as a dietician at her own business. Isabel married and has two children; she worked as a physical therapist for a few years and eventually became a hospital administrator. Julia became a principal, married, and has three children. Maria married and has one child; she works as a school guidance counselor. Emilia eventually married her college sweetheart; she coordinates a church youth program, is in the reserves, and works in international business relations.

REFERENCES

1. Niebuhr, Reinhold. *Serenity Prayer.*
2. Gillilan, Strickland. *As I Go On My Way.*
3. Wood, Jeff. "Side by Side." *Vintage Collection,* performed by Heritage Singers, 2018.
4. White, Ellen. *Adventist Home.* Review and Herald Publishing Association, 1952.
5. White, Ellen. *The Ministry of Healing.* Pacific Press Publishing Association, 1905.
6. White, Ellen. "The Importance of Expressing Gratitude and Praise." *Review and Harold,* 2 June 1910.
7. Jule Creaser. "When morning breaks and I face the day."
8. Author Unknown. *Plan of the Master Weaver.*
9. Poole, William C. Just *When I Need Him Most.*

CPSIA information can be obtained
at www.ICGtesting.com
Printed in the USA
LVHW030613170321
681672LV00010B/117

9 781736 010303